Your Guide to Self-Directed IRA Retirement Investing

FROM WALL STREET
TO MAIN STREET SERIES

Disclaimer: The book does not provide details or infer the procedure of real estate investments, or other alternative asset investments, or other associated tax and/or legal information. If you decide to choose that investment path, we recommend that you consult with an accredited self-directed IRA advisor, CPA and/or legal counsel for your specific situation. This book does not promise, imply or in anyway state any level or degree of investment success.

ISBN 978-0-6152-2308-7

Asset Exchange Strategies Publishing, LLC

Created and Printed in the United States of America

TO MY PARENTS

To my mother who truly believed that her son hung the moon. She never met a person who did not like her or wanted to share her as their Mom. She truly laid the foundation upon which all of my self-esteem is built upon; and,

To my father who taught me to dream big, create and accomplish goals and stay the course. No one had two parents who loved their children as much as they do.

TESTIMONIALS

"**Dan is the nation's reigning strategist** on asset exchange and self-directed retirement investment" Scott Janko, President, National Association Estate Planning

"**Dan was pretty aggressive** about getting out there and he was truly ahead of the curve. And because of the LLC I was able to make a $55,000 investment and 16 months later went up to $83,000." Darin Davis, CEO, Captuity Investments, Inc.

"**Investments through my IRA LLC enabled me** to purchase another gas station, another restaurant and a car wash" Harry, Entrepreneur, California.

" **After meeting Dan Cordoba, I realized** he was the one we needed to create an alliance. For many years, Sage International, Inc. was a pioneer in the formation of Self-Directed IRA LLC's because we understood and believed in the benefits of Self-Directed Investing. With all of the changes, knowledge and expertise required to keep up, I had to make a decision: Either we stop providing them because it was getting harder to support our clients or I needed to find someone we could work with who could handle all of the set up and ongoing support required for our clients. It's been great because his company does all of the work, but more important was his personal mission to educate the masses about the availability of this tool.

There is real power in his message: You get to control your own financial destiny and not somebody else!" Cheri S. Hill, President & CEO, Sage International, Inc. Reno NV

"**Dan Cordoba is an idea man**. For example, if he sees a glass on the table he'll think about how to make it better, then find a market and sell it. Dan has really done his homework and his research is phenomenal" Jeremy Farver, AEG

CONTENTS

PREFACE

While this book focuses on investing your IRA retirement (or a portion of) in real estate, the information and guidance provided could be applied to self-directed investments not only in real estate, but also in tax liens, notes and mortgages, buying or capitalizing a franchise, another type of business, and funding your business idea.

INTRODUCTION

The "Raymond" portrayed in this book is a fictional character created to symbolize a new investor. This book is intended for the Raymond's of the investment world; investors who have some experience in investing Individual Retirement Account funds, but have not walked the entire nine yards into the heart of investment possibilities.

Throughout this book there is the mantra of the following benefits you will enjoy with your self-directed retirement account:

Absolute investment decision authority – you have self-directed control without custodial intervention, review fees or delays

Checkbook control – you have the ability to write your own checks without custodial fees

No asset value fee - you pay a fixed, small annual custodial fee regardless of your success

Litigation protection – you get the LLC structure that makes litigation against the retirement account very difficult.

The book does not provide details about the procedure of real estate investments, alternative asset investments, or other associated legal information. If you decide to choose that investment path, we strongly recommend that you consult with a genuine self-directed IRA advisor.

NOTE FROM THE AUTHOR

From the age of 16 as a door-to-door salesman for Fuller Brush, I've felt the pulse of my customers. Thinking outside the box has proven to create extraordinary benefits for my customers is continually rewarding to me.

When I began my working career in the Silicon Valley, I turned corporate champion recruited by "ailing" companies needing a solution to their manufacturing dilemmas. After my tenure with technology companies, I began a new self-employed career in the competitive world of mergers, acquisitions, and financial services. In 2000, one of my clients queried me about buying a property with IRA funds. That query became my mission to create strategies for self-directed investment of IRA funds. I wanted to help the average person with a little money make more money.

I had no immediate followers, no screaming and swooning fans. My first marketing strategy was a placard at the intersection of 183 North and Anderson Mill road (Austin, TX). It read, "Buy real estate with your IRA, and contact Dan…" I excitedly presented my self-directed IRA investment strategy to interested respondents and realtors. I compiled a list of 30 companies and showed my audiences how to earn 15% in a bad market by making self-directed investments in these companies.

In 2003 after exhaustive research and a few tax attorneys later, I found solid ground for my self-directed strategy in an IRA LLC. After that there was no turning back. I sold my first IRA LLC in 2003 and founded Asset Exchange that same year.

I take pride in an extreme makeover of traditional investment structures and clients; our clients receive investment returns ranging from 20% to 400%. However, I haven't stopped. I continue to contribute to the self-directed IRA investment community through articles and seminars; our articles are published in various city business journals, the Wall Street Journal, Business Week, ABC World News, Kiplinger's, Forbes and many other local and regional periodicals. We hold seminars across the nation tailored to individuals, real estate agents, financial planners and investors.

We thank all our clients who have provided investment testimonies that are described in this book, as well as our editors, Jasmine Pabby and Ramona Kar.

I still enjoy assisting future wealth builders such as you to meet their investment goals!

Best regards,

Dan Cordoba, CEA

Principal, Asset Exchange Group, LLC

Founder, Asset Exchange Strategies LLC

"I try to learn from the past, but I plan for the future by focusing exclusively on the present"

Donald Trump

"Nothing splendid has ever been achieved except by those who dared believe that something inside them was superior to circumstance"

Bruce Barton

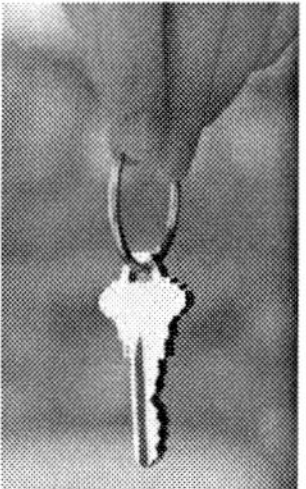

THE SUCCESSFUL MONEY STORY

"I had my IRA money in my investment account. Since I've moved it to my self-directed investment account I am now in control. I do not have another lost opportunity and I am ready for the next market downsize." Darin Davis, CEO Captuity Investments, Inc.

MEET DARIN

Darin Davis, CEO of Captuity Investments Firm, Inc. and a successful writer of his own money story. With $83,000 profits in his wallet he has a resume to be proud of.

"Because of the IRA LLC I was able to take a $55,000 investment and 18 months later make up to $83,000 in profit. That $83,000 has allowed me to go into two other investments, which will make significant returns. I attribute all of it to being able to do that first deal with the IRA LLC", Darin

Darin is a very versatile investor. He invests his self-directed IRA in real estate as well as in oil and gas, drawing from his previous experience with both types of investments. The applause owed to Darin is not only because of his lucrative winnings, but his willingness to examine new investment options, research them extensively, and discard the lead weight of fear. Darin has found a way not only to help his money grow wings, but a way to keep them soaring high.

Darin's Road to Victory

Darin didn't directly land on the victory lap. He had to journey there. In March 2000 he was on the precipice of a chasm, overlooking the grim scene on Wall Street. Corporate scandals, stock market downfalls, political upheavals, election seesaws, financial gloom and doom loomed large.

As he looked around for a lifeline to pull away from this fog and see the big picture, he was struck by two facts:

- Most people who were making good money were doing so outside the stock market through non-traditional investments (real estate, oil, gas).
- Unlike popular belief, IRA funds were not dead money. People tended to remain with traditional investments (stocks, bonds), because they worried about incurring penalties if they invested their IRA funds non-traditionally.

Not willing to let his IRA sit idle any longer, Darin began researching how these funds could best be used and found the answer in a mechanism called "self-directed IRA", a tool tailored for investments in non-traditional assets.

"As an active, aggressive investor I wanted to find a way I could better manage my IRA contributions, the admin and time delay and paper work it involved. Also, the issues I faced with my then current custodian were costing me opportunities. So I had a lot of lost opportunity costs." Darin

In 2003, Darin met Daniel Cordoba, CEA, Founder and President of the Asset Exchange Group. Hard work in the previous years with self-directed IRAs was paying off, and potential clients were viewing Dan as the self-directed IRA expert and Knowledge Leader in the industry.

Darin was introduced to an IRA LLC, a customized lifeline that frees IRA investors from the shackles of custodian constraints and empowers them to direct their own investments in compliance with IRS codes.

This became Darin's lifeline to investment victory. It enabled him to:

- Invest in deals with his IRA funds without ever having to ask his custodian's permission.
- Write checks immediately without waiting for them to arrive from his custodian.

Winning Boost

Darin is deliberate in what he does. He is very thorough in investigating the processes involved. He grills with questions, involves his attorney and other advisors in his research, and studies the whole scenario in detail.

"I couldn't risk a few hundred thousand in my IRA so I consulted my attorney who went through the IRA LLC paperwork pretty closely. It was pretty aggressive and Dan was truly ahead of the curve." Darin

Darin was skeptical at first. We worked with him for more than three months to show him that embracing the IRA LLC as a lifeline was worth it. A fateful event finally clinched it for Darin - he lost out on a lucrative deal because it took his custodian a long time to send the check that he needed to close the deal. Ironically this loss was the winning boost that he needed. It propelled him into buying an IRA LLC.

Darin currently sells IRA LLC's; his company is an affiliate of Asset Exchange Strategies. This relationship allows his company to educate, train, and find assets for his clients to invest in, while Asset Exchange Group provides the IRA LLC to make the investment.

Darin has just bought an IRA LLC for his wife, and will be doing the same for his mom at the end of the year.

ANOTHER SUCCESSFUL MONEY STORY

Another successful advising journey is Mike Springer, an Agent at Global Realty Marketing. Mike was working with a traditional custodian and his biggest frustration was caused by expensive custodian-driven delays. When he bought property and wanted to repair and remodel it, he had to wait weeks in order to receive checks from his custodian.

We showed Mike how he could best use his self-directed IRA funds through an IRA LLC. Mike thoroughly enjoyed the checkbook control that the IRA LLC offered. It became his lifeline.

"My goal is to create equity every time I purchase. For example, I buy a home for $60,000, invest $10,000 to turn it around, and sell it for $100,000. You can't make this much with stocks. I am totally satisfied." Mike Springer, Agent, Global Realty Marketing

CREATE YOUR OWN MONEY STORY

Your fingerprints cannot be duplicated. Your dreams, loves, passions, fears, longings, plans cannot be photocopied. You have a journey that only you can map. You impact the world uniquely.

But with all your uniqueness you share common needs, the most important of them being food, clothing, shelter, safety, love, belonging, esteem, and self-actualization (Abraham Maslow). Money is one of the tools available to us to help meet these needs and you have your own "money story", and "money journey" that you create.

Thanks to the Employee Retirement Security Act (ERISA), most of us have a pouch of money to begin with, and our own mental blueprint of where we'd like to see it go. One option is to whistle for your own personal genie and make a wish. A more practical option is to plot your own journey, fueled by knowledge of your investment options, fired by zeal for more control of your investment paths, and empowered by the support and experience of trusted advisors.

The overall message is that you have the choice of where your money is invested and how your retirement fund is managed.

Bringing the "Would" Bridge to You

The advising journeys with Darin and Mike are very typical of the thousands of IRA holders seeking a different investment path with an IRA LLC.

In these and other journeys as a self-directed IRA advisor, we observed investors often find themselves thrust into a chasm by various investment-related factors including ignorance of available options, tax code terrors, misleading advice, custodian constraints, and other financial fears. That's when we designed the "Would Bridge," an icon that spans the gap from traditional to non-traditional investments. A self-directed advisor's role is to help investors identify their own entry point out of the chasm and on to the bridge, and like Darin and Mike, learn to create their own lifeline and weave their own path across.

Crossing this bridge does not mean that you have to travel in a straight line towards self-directed IRA investments. You may decide that staying with traditional investments may work best for you.

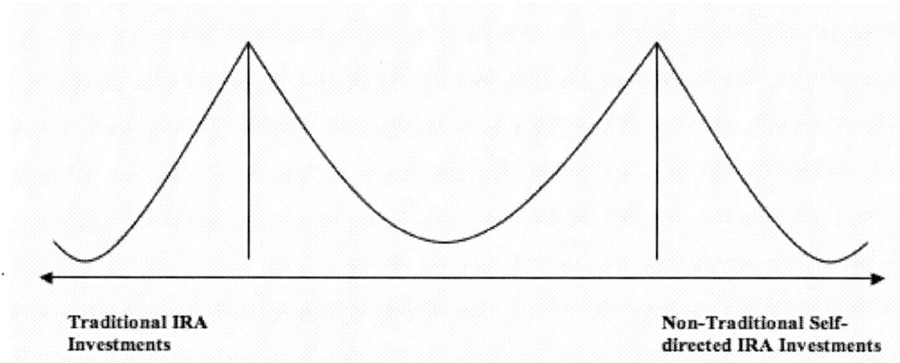

However, don't make that decision without exploring the non-traditional investment opportunity and then make an informed choice.

Lets follow that decision path with what we can call "a typical investor" as he journeys to the side of non-traditional self-directed IRA investment.

Meet Raymond ..... 

√ Summary Check List

- Good money can be made through non-traditional investments.
- Self-directed investing allows you to decide where your IRA funds will be invested: You are always in control.
- The role of the self-directed Advisor is to help the investor enter the self-directed investing arena.

"High achievers spot rich opportunities swiftly, make big decisions quickly and move into action immediately. Follow these principles and you can make your dreams come true"

Robert H. Schuller

"The most successful men in the end are those whose success is the result of steady accretion... It is the man who carefully advances step by step, with his mind becoming wider and wider - and progressively better able to grasp any theme or situation - persevering in what he knows to be practical, and concentrating his thought upon it, who is bound to succeed in the greatest degree"

Alexander Graham Bell

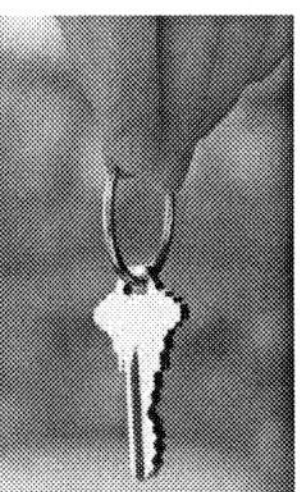

JOURNEY TOWARDS NON-TRADITIONAL INVESTMENTS

"I want to know what I am getting into. What are my options? What is the process? Is this process for me? Is it safe? Will I be in trouble if I use my IRA the way I want? What about the IRS?" Raymond, new investor

---

PATH TO SUCCESS

Raymond is also keen on successfully writing his money story. He knows what he wants but isn't exactly sure how to get there. He has experimented with different IRA investment strategies but is extremely dissatisfied with the outcome. He hands over money from his traditional IRA to his custodian who makes investment choices for him. He initially feels content to let the experts handle his IRA funds, but soon grows frustrated with their narrow investment playing field.

As he becomes more knowledgeable about IRA investments he wants a wider playing field. At his request, his custodian lets him choose the stocks, bonds, or mutual funds in which he invests his money. He feels a little better knowing where his money went.

However, the erratic stock market took its toll and Raymond found himself in a financial chasm. He learns about alternative investment opportunities that are not securities- related; investments that would let him invest his IRA funds in non-traditional assets. But his IRA funds are his life savings and he simply cannot afford to risk them to a concept that he does not know too much about. Doubts, fears, and queries all threatened to overshadow his enthusiasm.

When we first meet Raymond, we realize the need to address his fears through sound knowledge, ensure that he makes an informed decision through due diligence, along with providing inspiration through successful client testimonies. We integrated all three prongs of The IRA LLC Learning Process to provide a strong anchor to Raymond against doubts and fears.

A LEARNING PROCESS

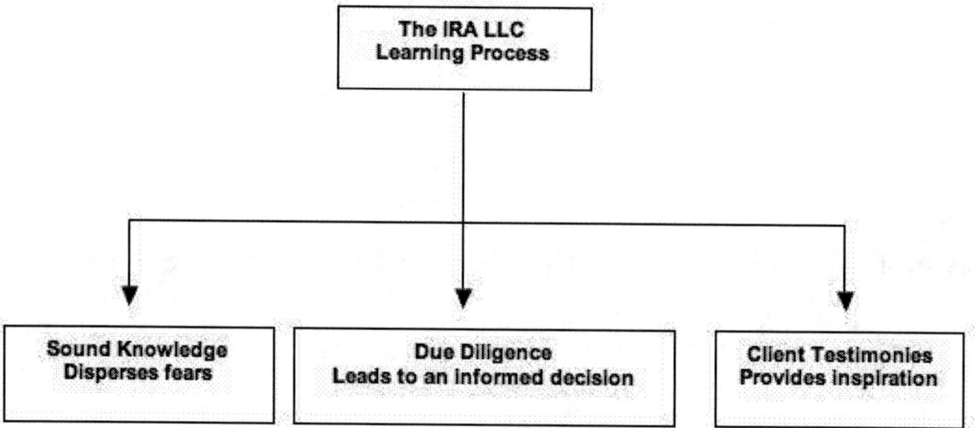

Sound Knowledge

Raymond must grasp investment concepts from simple to complex, and from tried and tested to brand new. He needs these stepping-stones to integrate this knowledge of the IRA and IRA LLC.

Raymond needs to understand:

- The genuine self-directed IRA
- An IRA LLC
- What the IRS cares about
- The importance of a self-directed advisor
- The importance of due-diligence

Due diligence

Due-diligence is a "hawk's eye" test applied in advance of any decision to invest, enter into a partnership, or start a business venture. Due-diligence involves research, analysis, review, and investigation into possible risks: an important ongoing process. The information he collects through this process will help him make an informed decision about choosing an advisor and determining the best type of transaction for his investment needs.

Use of "How to Conduct a Meaningful Due-Diligence Investigation" guide, created by Asset Exchange Group helps him through all the steps of this process.

After all, it's Raymond's money: he worked hard for every penny of it. It's time he has veto power over his IRA investments. But where does he begin the journey?

Client Testimonies

Raymond reviews several client testimonies and personally meets some of the clients. This provides a confidence booster for him and motivates him to begin his journey.

√ Summary Check List

- Sound knowledge disperses new self-directed investor fears.
- Due-diligence leads to an informed investment decision.
- Client testimonies provide inspiration to self-directed investors.

"So what do we do? Anything. Something. So long as we just don't sit there. If we screw it up, start over. Try something else. If we wait until we've satisfied all the uncertainties, it may be too late"

Lee Iacocca

"You see, in life, lots of people know what to do, but few people actually do what they know. Knowing is not enough! You must take action"

Anthony Robbins

RAYMOND AND HIS IRA

"The investments permitted in an IRA include virtually every financial product or vehicle on the market." John J. Scavuzzo, Real Estate Broker and Author of The Real Estate IRA, published in 1987

Raymond holds in his hands a vibrant tool: the individual retirement account (IRA) brought into being by the Retirement Security Act (ERISA) in 1974. He knows that whether traditional or non-traditional, his investment assets are a mere shell without the IRA. But to fully exploit the potential of his IRA; he needs to get to know his IRA like the back of his hand.

Even though he has some experience with IRA investments, and has learned about new IRA concepts through research and various seminars, he first needs to return to the drawing board and update his knowledge on the fundamentals of an IRA.

He can surf the web, browse library shelves, and research the IRS website to update his IRA data bank.

We then supplemented the information with a snapshot review of the different IRA types.

IRA Types

The IRA is funded by yearly contributions based on pre-determined contribution limits. Following are the various types of IRAs, most of which are based on the Traditional or Roth model:

- Traditional IRA
- Roth IRA
- Spousal IRA
- Inherited IRA
- Simple IRA
- SEP IRA
- Education Savings Account IRA
- Health Savings Account IRA

Traditional IRA

How do you contribute to a Traditional IRA?

- Wages
- Salary
- Tips
- Commission

- Self-employment (including self employment not subject to tax because of religious beliefs)
- Alimony? Really?
- Scholarship and fellowship compensation

How do you set up a Traditional IRA?

- At a bank or financial institution; or
- Through mutual funds; or
- With a stockbroker
- For a self-directed IRA: www.trausteeamerica.com

What else should you know about a Traditional IRA?

- Has a specified limit on contributions – contribution deadline is usually April 15.
- Has no restriction on how often or when you make contributions. File Form 8606 if you make non-deductible contributions.
- Taxes any investments and earnings at the time of early withdrawal prior to 59½ years. If you make a withdrawal before 59½, you pay a 10% penalty along with federal and state taxes (total tax liability = IRA withdrawal + total income for the year). Refer to IRA Rollovers for more information on avoiding tax penalties.
- Permits penalty-free withdrawals after 59½.

- Requires initial mandatory withdrawals at 70½. You are also charged penalties if you fail to start withdrawals by April 1 following the year you become 70½. To calculate the minimum withdrawal from your IRA after age 70½, refer to Publication 590, Individual Retirement Arrangements (IRAs).
- Allow both partners in a marriage to contribute even if only one partner was employed during the year. The employed partner must have earned enough to cover the contributions for both individuals.
- Lets you create a separate Traditional IRA for children who earn from employment. Other family members also can contribute up to the full allowable amount for each year.

What are the contribution limits for a Traditional IRA?

The IRS does allow for early distribution without penalty. See your self-directed IRA Advisor since these rules are very specific and if not handled properly could result in large penalties.

However, it may be the perfect tool for those that need to buy an investment for themselves another disqualified person to use.

Tax Year	Contributions ($) for Age < 50	Contributions ($) for Age 50+
2005	4000	4500
2006	4000	5000
2007	4000	5000
2008	5000	6000

What are the exceptions for early withdrawals?

- Extreme medical expenses, and permanently disabled
- Health insurance premiums in certain circumstances
- First-time homebuyers
- Higher education expenses in certain circumstances
- Death
- Equal distributions based on life expectancy

ROTH IRA

The Roth IRA, created by the Tax Payer Relief Act (1997), lets you:

- Invest after tax money even after 70½.
- Enjoy the earnings and principal contribution tax-free upon withdrawal.

▶ **Note**: Both partners in a marriage can contribute, even if only one partner was employed during the year. The employed partner must have earned enough to cover the contributions for both individuals.

You must file Form 8606 if you received distributions from a Roth IRA except for a rollover, re-characterization, qualified distributions, or a return of certain distributions.

What withdrawal restrictions you should be aware of?

To avoid penalties and taxes, you can make withdrawals only when:

- Substantially Equal Periodic Payments (SEPP)
- Five years have elapsed since the IRA was first established, and
- The owner is 59½ years or more, has become disabled, or is deceased and the beneficiary receives the assets.

What are the contribution limits for a Roth IRA?

Tax Year	**Contributions ($) for Age < 50**	**Contributions ($) for Age 50 +**
2005	4000	4500
2006	4000	5000
2007	4000	5000
2008	5000	6000

Where is the Magic in a Roth?

- You contribute after-tax money.
- The Roth grows tax-free and is not taxed upon distribution.
- There is no minimum limit on distributions, so you determine the amount to be withdrawn.

▶ **Note**: The Roth IRA may also be passed onto heirs without taxation.

Which Should You Invest in - Roth or Traditional IRA?

For both Traditional and Roth IRA
• You must have earned income. • You must contribute according to specific limits. • You can contribute for a non-working spouse. • You must contribute by April 15 of the following year. • You can accept rollovers from other IRAs. • Your earnings grow tax-deferred. • You pay an early withdrawal penalty with exceptions. • You can avoid probate. • You may be subject to estate taxes. • Your beneficiaries can continue the tax deferral.

For Traditional IRA
• Your contribution is tax deductible. • You can accept rollovers from non- IRA pension plans. • Your withdrawals are not tax-free. • You must begin withdrawing by 59 ½. • You cannot contribute after 70 ½. Your beneficiary has to pay income tax (applies to certain income levels only).
For Roth IRA
• Your contribution is non-tax deductible. • You cannot accept rollovers from non-IRA pension plans (in 2008 you can accept). • Your withdrawals are tax-free. • You can withdraw five years after the IRA is first established and if you are 59 ½ years or more. For additional restrictions, refer to what withdrawal restrictions must you be careful of. • You are not mandated to withdraw and your earnings can continue to grow tax-free. • You can contribute after 70 ½. Your beneficiary does not have to pay income tax.

SPOUSAL IRA

You can set up the Spousal IRA in three easy steps for a spouse who is not employed, or earns little or no income:

- Open the account in your spouse's name;
- Use your spouse's social security number; and
- Name yourself as beneficiary.

If you divorce, the IRA can be transferred between spouses through:

- A rollover, or
- Change of name on the IRA by court order.

▶ **Note**: A spousal IRA does not imply that both partners own the same IRA (each person owns their own IRA account).

What else should you know about a Spousal IRA?

To be eligible, you and your spouse must be legally married at the end of the tax year; you must also:

- File a joint income tax return.
- Be employed.
- Have earned an income greater than or equal to the contribution.
- Be 70 ½ years or less for a traditional IRA, the Roth IRA has no age limit.

- If you set up a traditional IRA there are no limits on the amount you earn.
- If you set up a Roth IRA, your earnings must not exceed $160,000.
- If your adjusted gross income (AGI) is less than $150,000 and you have a retirement plan, the Spousal IRA is fully deductible.
- If your AGI is between $150,000 and $160,000, the Spousal IRA is partially deductible.

▶ **Note**: In 2010 anyone can convert to a traditional IRA to a Roth IRA regardless of income level.

You can take advantage of:

- Catch-up contribution limit if you and your spouse are over 50; and
- Tax deduction for the current tax year, if you open the IRA before April 15 of the following year.

What are the contribution limits for a Spousal IRA?

Tax Year	Contributions
2005	If your spouse if over 50, an additional $500
2006-2008	If your spouse if over 50, an additional $1,000
2005 2006 2007	The lesser of the amounts earned, or $4,000
2008	The lesser of the amounts earned, or $5,000

INHERITED IRA

What do you do if you inherit from your spouse? You can:

- Treat the IRA as your own by designating yourself as the account owner; or
- Roll it over into your traditional IRA or other qualified plan, see Publication 590, page 18, for information; or
- Treat yourself as the beneficiary rather than treating the IRA as your own.

If you decide to treat the IRA as your own, you:

- Must contribute (including rollover contributions) to the IRA; or
- Must not take the required minimum distribution for a year as a beneficiary of the IRA.

You must also:

- Be the sole beneficiary of the IRA; and
- Have an unlimited right to withdraw money from it.

You can choose to begin receiving distributions:

- On the date when your spouse would have reached 70½, or

- By December 31 of the calendar year following the year in which your spouse died.

▶ **Note:** You do not owe taxes until after you start-receiving distributions. For additional information see Publication 590, page 33.

What should you do if you inherit a Traditional IRA from someone other than your spouse?

There are restrictions on treating the IRA as your own. But you can choose any of the following two options:

- Transfer the IRA to an Inherited IRA Beneficiary Distribution Account; those who share the inheritance must set up their own accounts within certain time frames for each portion of the inheritance; or
- Disclaim all or part of your portion of the IRA within nine months of the owner's death.

SIMPLE IRA

A Simple IRA plan is a tax-favorable retirement plan that certain small employers (including self-employed individuals) can set up for their employees. For additional information on employer requirements, see Publication 560.

The Simple plan is a written agreement between you and your employer in which you agree to have:

- Your compensation reduced by a certain percentage each pay period; and
- Your salary reductions transferred to a SIMPLE IRA on your behalf.

▶ **Note**: The Simple IRA is based on the Traditional IRA model.

What should you do to be eligible?

Even if self-employed, you must:

- Receive at least $5,000 in compensation from your employer during any two years before the current year; and
- Reasonably expect to receive at least $5,000 in compensation during the calendar year for which contributions are made.

You can be excluded if:

- Your retirement benefits are covered by a collective bargaining agreement; or
- You are a non-resident alien and received no earned income from sources within the United States.

What are the other benefits?

- You enjoy higher tax-deferred contributions than either the Traditional or the Roth IRA.
- You can be part of a 401K plan.
- You receive plan benefits that are portable because the funding is held entirely in an IRA for you.

- You can own your account and are always 100% vested.
- You can choose to match employer contributions.
- You can make non-elective contributions (up to 2% of salary) rather than match contributions.
- You can convert a SIMPLE IRA to a Roth IRA after a qualifying period (two years after the first employer contributions).

What's the catch?

- You must make significant regular contributions for the SIMPLE IRA to serve as an adequate retirement shelter; and
- Your annual contributions are usually restricted to lesser amounts than with a qualified 401K or 403B plan (e.g. 2003 limits were $8,000 for a SIMPLE plan and $12,000 for a 401K or 403B plan).

What are the contribution limits for a Simple IRA?

Tax Year	Contributions ($) for Age < 50	Contributions ($) for Age 50 +
2005	10,000	2,000
2006	10,000	2,500
2007	10,000	2,500
2008	10,000	2,500

▶ **Note**: For additional information, see Publication 560, page 9.

SEP- IRA

The SEP-IRA plan is a formal, written agreement that lets your employer make contributions toward your retirement. This IRA applies to self-employed individuals too. As the employee, you own and control the SEP–IRA.

What should you do to be eligible?

You must:

- Be at least 21 years;
- Have worked for the employer for at least three of the last five years; and
- Have received at least $450 in compensation from the employer for 2005.

▶ **Note**: Contributions once deposited become Traditional IRA assets governed by many of the Traditional IRA rules.

You can be excluded if:

- Your retirement benefits are covered by a collective bargaining agreement; or
- You are a non-resident alien and received no earned income from sources within the United States.

What must your employer do?

- Contribute a limited amount of money each year to your IRA. The employer receives a tax deduction for the contribution for the tax year in which the contribution is made.
- Route your contributions through the financial institution that maintains the SEP-IRA.
- Establish and make SEP contributions by the due date of the federal income tax return of the business, including extensions.
- Make SEP contributions directly without incurring payroll taxes.
- May reduce contributions or even skip a year penalty-free, if profits are small.

What are the contribution limits for a SEP-IRA?

For 2005, the maximum contribution is the lesser of the following:

- 25% of each employee's compensation; or
- $42,000.

▶ **Note**: For additional information see Publication 560, page 6.

COVERDELL EDUCATION SAVINGS ACCOUNT (ESA)

This is a trust or savings account created to pay qualified education expenses at an eligible educational institution for a designated account beneficiary.

▶ **Note:** For detailed definitions of "qualified education expenses" and "eligible education institution" refer to Publication 970, pages 39 and 40.

What requirements must you meet as a beneficiary?

You must be under 18 when the ESA is created or a special needs beneficiary. The account custodian must be a bank or IRS-approved entity.

Who contributes and how must they contribute?

Anyone including a corporation or trust or you can make contributions. The contributor's modified adjusted gross income for the year must be less than $110,000, or $220,000 in case of a joint return.

Contributions are not tax-deductible, and must be made:

- In cash; and
- By the due date of the contributor's tax return excluding extensions.

Money in the account cannot be:

- Invested in life insurance contracts; and
- Combined with other property, except in a common trust or investment fund.

What are the contribution limits for an ESA IRA?

For 2005, there are two yearly limits that apply to the beneficiary and the contributor:

- As a beneficiary, you can receive up to a total of $2,000 toward your Coverdell ESA regardless of the number of contributors. e.g., if three persons contribute, their total contribution cannot exceed $2,000 per ESA, and
- Each contributor can contribute only up to $2,000 toward each ESA. e.g. if one person contributes to two siblings' ESAs, each contribution must not exceed $2,000.

How do I receive the money?

You can receive a distribution at any time. The distribution is usually tax-free provided it does not exceed your adjusted qualified educational expenses for the year. The earnings on the account grow tax-free until distributed. You do not have to be enrolled for a minimum number of courses to take a tax-free distribution.

After you complete your education at an eligible educational institution, the account balance must be distributed within 30 days after the earlier of the following events when you reach 30, unless you are a special needs beneficiary, or your death.

▶ **Note**: For additional information, refer to Publication 970, pages 41-48.

HEALTH SAVINGS ACCOUNT (HSA)

An HSA is set up as a tax-exempt trust or custodial account with a qualified HSA trustee (bank, insurance company, or anyone approved by the IRS to be an IRA trustee). Its intent is to reimburse qualified medical expenses you incur. The trustee need not be your health plan provider.

How do I qualify for an HSA? You must:

- Have a high deductible health plan (HDHP) on the first day of the month;
- Have no other health coverage except what is permitted under "Other Health Coverage";
- Not be enrolled under Medicare; and
- Not be claimed as a dependent on someone else's 2005 tax return.

▶ **Note**: For a definition of "qualified medical expenses" and "high deductible health plan" refer to Publication 969, pages 2 and 6.

What does Other Health Coverage include?

Additional insurance that provides benefits for:

- Liabilities incurred under workers' compensation laws, tort liabilities, or ownership or property liabilities;
- A specific disease or illness; or
- Hospitalization (a fixed amount per day (or other period)); and
- It also includes coverage for accidents, disability, dental care, vision care, and long-term care.

▶ **Note**: For additional information on High Deductible Health Plan, refer to Publication 969, pages 2 and 3.

What are the contribution limits for an HSA IRA?

Contributions must be in cash, and can be made by any eligible individuals, including the following:

- An employer or employee, or both can contribute in the same year toward an employee's HSA.
- Self-employed or unemployed individuals can contribute toward their own HSA.
- Family members or any other person can contribute on behalf of an eligible individual.

The contribution amount depends on:

- Type of your HDHP coverage, and your age.
- For 2005, if you have coverage only for self, you can contribute up to the amount of your annual health plan deductible but not more than $2,650. If you have family coverage, you can contribute up to the amount of your annual health plan deductible but not more than $5,250.
- Report all HSA contributions on Form 8889, Health Savings Account and file it with Form 1040.

▶ **Note**: For additional information on contribution limits, Rules for Married People, and Form 8889 instructions, refer to Publication 969, pages 4 and 5.

Distributions

You can receive tax-free distributions from your HSA to pay or be reimbursed for your qualified medical expenses. These expenses are those that will not be reimbursed by your HDHP.

IRA Rollover

A rollover occurs when you withdraw cash or other assets from one eligible retirement plan and contribute all or part of it within 60 days to another eligible retirement plan. A rollover is not taxable but it is reportable on your federal tax return.

▶ **Note**: Any taxable distribution paid to you is subject to a mandatory withholding of 20%, even if you intend to roll it over later.

You can do a rollover either by requesting your employer to:

- Directly roll over the plan payout into a Rollover IRA, and thus help you avoid the 20% IRS withholding tax, or
- Give you a check for the rollover amount; you can then deposit the check plus 20% into a rollover IRA within 60 days, and avoid the 20% IRS withholding tax.

For further information about rollovers and transfers, refer to:

- Tax Topic 413: www.irs.gov/taxtopics/tc413.html
- Publication 575: www.irs.gov/publications/p575/ar02.html#d0e3603
- Publication 590, pages 22, 23, 24 and 59.

√ Summary Check List

- Before you embark in self-directed investing understand:
    - Your IRA choices
    - The IRA's entry, distribution, and exiting rules
    - A self-directed IRA is the same as an IRA with a broker except the asset is different
    - All of these plans can be self-directed

"Money talks...but all mine ever says is good-bye"

Anon

"The assumption must be that those who can see value only in tradition, or versions of it, deny man's ability to adapt to changing circumstances"

Stephen Bayley

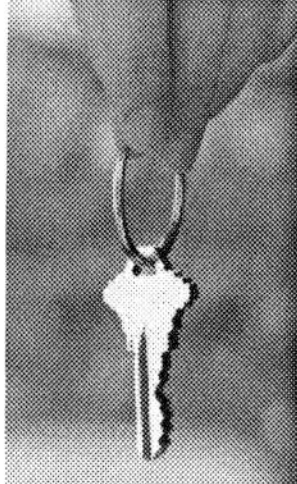

IRA BENEFITS

Raymond concludes the bottom line would be regardless of whether he remained with traditional IRA investments, or chooses the non-traditional path the following benefits would be his.

TAX-DEFERRED COMPOUNDING INTEREST

One of the greatest benefits of an IRA is the power of tax-deferred compounding interest or interest on interest. For example, a return on any investment allows you to enjoy interest on both the investment principle and the accumulated earnings. The additional interest you make on profits is compound interest. But because of an IRA's tax-deferred status you can defer tax on your earnings and benefit from compounding on all your profits, not just what is left after tax.

FAVORABLE TAX BENEFITS WITH A ROTH IRA

With a Roth IRA, you contribute with after-tax dollars so although you do not receive a deduction, your profits are tax-free. When your investment appreciates and cash flow increases you can reinvest tax-free into other assets and diversify your portfolio.

TRADITIONAL IRAS REDUCE TAXABLE INCOME

Contributions to a traditional IRA are tax deductible – income restrictions apply.

PENALTY-FREE EARLY DISTRIBUTIONS

In certain circumstances (certain health expenses, higher education expenses and first time home buyers) you are legally authorized to receive substantially equal periodic payments (SEPP) from your IRA before the age of 59 ½ with a minimum distribution period of 5 years.

IRAs HELP PROTECT ASSETS

In most states, IRAs have considerable protection against most creditors, excluding the IRS and spouses.

IRAs PROVIDE A GREAT PLANNING TOOL

Whether providing for a newborn or estate planning, there is nothing like an IRA.

Feeling more invigorated than ever before, Raymond decides to peel away the layers of traditional investment thinking and stamp his own identity on his IRA income.

INVESTMENT PLAN COMPARISON CHART

Visit our web site at www.

√ Summary Check List

- IRA's provide five dynamic benefits:
    - Tax-deferred compounding interest
    - Reduce taxable income
    - Penalty free distributions
    - Protect assets
    - Great planning tool
- Remember just like investing in a stock, the non-traditional investment appreciation is a gain and not a contribution!

"Always bear in mind that your own resolution to succeed is more important than any other one thing"

Abraham Lincoln

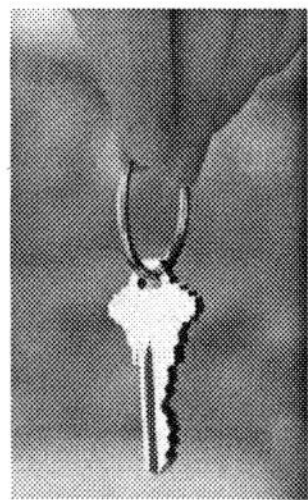

UNDERSTANDING GENUINE SELF-DIRECTED IRA

"No IRA advisor can stamp my identity on my IRA. I've got to decide how far I want to travel with my IRA, what risks I am willing to take, and whom to trust",

Raymond, new investor

FIRST THINGS FIRST

Raymond first needs to understand the difference between self-directed IRA and a genuine Self-Directed IRA.

Self-directed IRA	Genuine self-directed IRA
IRA owners choose a traditional asset (stock, bond, or mutual fund) in which to invest their IRA funds. The choice of asset is limited to their custodian's group of stocks, bonds, and mutual funds.	IRA owners choose their own traditional or non-traditional assets, e.g. CDs, securities, annuities, real estate, oil and gas, tax liens. The IRA owner decides the type of asset in which to invest and therefore is truly in control.

Raymond also needs to carefully study the providers in the self-directed IRA market before making a choice. He has learned that per IRS rules you must enlist a custodian when investing your IRA funds.

The providers include:

- IRA custodian or administrator offers investment products and holds and reports investments to the IRS, but cannot offer advice, e.g., Charles Schwab Fidelity.
- Attorney group offers legal advice on IRAs and ensures that the deal is set up correctly.
- Self-directed IRA advisor, e.g. Asset Exchange Group (AEG) offers investment products, strategies, and advice on self-directed IRAs and IRA LLC's.

▶ **Note:** Even if you sign up with a self-directed IRA advisor, you still need a custodian to hold and report your assets to the IRS.

Is My IRA Genuinely Self-directed?

It was Raymond's job to critically scrutinize his IRA investments and put it to the genuine self-directed IRA test by asking these questions:

1. Who drives my decision regarding where, when, and how to invest my IRA funds – my custodian or me?

2. Do I feel restricted by the investment choices offered by my custodian?
3. Am I able to diversify my IRA investments to include non-traditional assets?
4. Has my custodian satisfactorily answered questions about non-traditional investments or did he or she merely discourage me about opting for this choice?
5. Has my custodian supported my exploratory steps toward non-traditional investments?
6. Do I feel confident about re-shaping my investments to meet my personal and financial goals?
7. Do I feel forced to play the stock market just because there is no other option?
8. Is my IRA building wealth for me?

Even without magical intervention, the writing on the wall was clear. Raymond's IRA is not genuinely self-directed. He revisits some of the successful client testimonies.

One of them was Philip and Jeanine King, owners of Lowell King Insurance Service, Bardwell Kentucky.

Their dad had done extensive Internet research and read about self-directed IRAs in the Wall Street Journal. "We bought 240 acres in a tree farm. We believe the value of this property will go up three times in five years. By investing in land, we are contributing more toward our retirement than by keeping the money in our Roth IRA and earning just 5%. If another September 11 occurs, the stock market will plummet. Trees are our future."

Philip and Jeanine reported that they were extremely happy with their self-directed IRA investments and just wished they had begun earlier. There optimism as well those of other AEG client's experiences combined with Raymond's own positive experiences spark his determination to turn his investment life around.

Along with the positives of transferring to a genuine self-directed IRA, Raymond also hears downsides. However, thanks to his research he is systematically able to distil the truth and weed out the misconceptions.

POSITIVE SELF-TALK

Raymond now knows better than to rush out and transfer his funds to a self-directed IRA. He reminds himself of all he had learned and reinforced his knowledge with positive self-talk.

▶ **"I'll have more investment choices and more investment control"**

That means that within IRA regulations, I can invest in real estate, foreclosures, tax certificates, mineral rights, businesses, private stock, notes, gold coins, REITS, tax liens, hedge funds, mutual funds. My self-directed IRA advisor will help me comply with the Prohibited Transactions rule. I'll be in the driver's seat from where I can choose investments, and decide if and when to buy or sell.

▶ "I can diversify my portfolio and ensure that my risk is minimized too"

Apart from life insurance and certain collectibles, I know that my genuine Self-Directed IRA can hold any kind of asset. I can diversify into other business areas. I have the option to roll over funds to a Self-Directed IRA LLC, and then spread my investments among both traditional and non-traditional assets.

This will help me maximize my earning potential and minimize my risks, as well as reduce my administrative overheads and associated fees. I will then be able to weather any investment climate from a bear market to a real estate crash.

By transferring only part of my existing IRA funds to a self-directed IRA, I wouldn't risk my entire retirement fund, even if my investments fail or my IRA is disqualified due to a prohibitive transaction.

"There is so much more money in real estate. Every time a person sells a house, that person's net worth increases. If you have undervalued assets, and then turn them around, you can create wealth. The downside is, you don't have to replace the roof of a stock. Diversification is an excellent idea." Mike Springer, Agent, Global Realty Marketing

▶ **"My Self-Directed IRA accepts transfers from several types of retirement accounts"**

Here are some of them: Traditional IRAs, Sep IRAs, Roth IRAs, 401(k)s, 403(b)s, Qualified Annuities, Profit Sharing Plans, Money Purchase Plans, Government Eligible Deferred Compensation Plans, and Keoghs.

▶ **"Real estate investments are an exciting prospect for me"**

I know I can legally purchase real estate with my self-directed IRA funds and direct any rental or capital profits back to my self-directed IRA. I can also use my self-directed IRA funds to pay for maintenance fees and development, decorative work, and upgrades or modernizations.

"With my self-directed IRA I can open the door to the most exciting investment tool of the 21st century - Self-Directed IRA LLC". My self-directed IRA advisor can facilitate the transfer of my current self-directed IRA funds to a self-directed IRA LLC, if I so desire.

▶ **"Best of all, I no longer view my IRA as a safety-net but as Wealth Builder"**

Because my IRA funds can now earn more returns, I can accumulate wealth in tangible assets. I can venture outside traditional IRA markets. I have the potential to triple and quadruple my self-directed IRA's value within a relatively short period of time. Philip and Jeanine King said that if they were able to sell their tree farm at their asking price, they would boost their IRA money by 250%. That is phenomenal to me!

▶ **"These misconceptions will not deter me!'**

Raymond will need to deal with naysayers too. With his new knowledge and inspiration from other investors he is able to easily disperse these misconceptions.

▶ **"The real estate market or my portfolio assets might fall."**

There is some risk just as with buying stocks and bonds. But as Daniel Cordoba, AEG Founder and President states in his seminar, economies don't fail universally.

When one segment goes down, another rises. Diversifying a portfolio will help offset any losses and often completely cancel out gains. Instead of buying and flipping. I can choose to hold property for a period of time, giving the market time to correct. Investments in notes or private mortgages provide an opportunity to invest in real estate while providing greater liquidity.

Investments can also be maneuvered in the direction of market changes. For example, in a down market I can purchase a non-traditional asset at a favorable price just as you would be able to purchase stock at a lower price in a bear market. On the other hand, if the stock market peaks and interest rates fall, real estate may be pushed up just as it did in the early 2000s, making it easy to choose it as an investment path.

▶ **"I have to be rich to invest."**

I can invest in all kinds of options e.g. private stock, REITs, tax liens, gold coins, etc, not just high-ticket purchases like real estate. For example, note brokering requires no funds to get started.

▶ **"It is too expensive to invest in real estate."**

I know it is prohibited to borrow money from my IRA, sell property to my IRA, receive unreasonable compensation for managing it, use my IRA as security for a loan, and buy property for personal use.

But none of these regulations prevent the investor from purchasing investment property outright with IRA funds, borrow money (through a non-recourse loan), or use another person's IRA in order to partially fund an investment. I can also take a low-cost option to buy a property within 60 days and, if I find a buyer at a higher price, I can make an immediate profit with little up-front cash.

▶ **"I must have all of the money in my IRA when purchasing the asset."**

I can also get a loan for the rest, put a small down payment on the property through the IRA, and take out the balance in a loan.

▶ **"Investing in non-traditional assets is too complex and expensive."**

I heard exactly the opposite! For example, if a potential investor knows how to buy used vehicles at an auction and turn those for a profit, then investing in non-traditional assets may be less risky than purchasing a mutual fund about which the investor may know little or nothing. I much prefer to invest a portion of my savings into something I do understand.

Using an IRA LLC, the annual custodial cost to hold the asset is very low and can be paid with IRA funds or out of pocket.

▶ "The genuine self-directed IRA concept is too new."

Not at all! After ERISA (1974)**,** the securities markets were the first to respond to IRA funding and the 401(k) market. At the time, banks and brokerage houses controlled the creation of the Plan Document so the only permissible assets were stocks, bonds and mutual funds. It was the crash of 2000 and the advent of the Internet that saw the birth of the genuine self-directed IRA market.

▶ "Investing in non-traditional assets is too risky."

Actually it is less uncertain than investing in the stock market. We've already heard experts say that non-traditional assets are more predictable and possibly more secure. For example notes are generally secured and the interest rate is predictable.

SELF-DIRECTED INVESTORS

Philip and Jeanine King wholeheartedly follow the non-traditional investment path with great results:

"We believe that investing in property, including farm land, condominiums, apartments, other rental property, is the most secure investment there is. The stock market may fall, but the value of the property stays. Even if it does go down, after a while it will come back. The population of the earth continues to increase; land will always stay the same. There are always people who are looking to buy property. You've got to create your own retirement. You've got to do it yourself," Philip King and Jeanine King.

End of Journey

Wow! Raymond has come a long way: from learning IRA types; to understanding what a genuine self-directed IRA is, to making a decision concerning his investment path.

Although he has crossed a major portion of the bridge, he believed that to reach the zenith of investment independence, he needed to explore further.

He became aware that there were still some hurdles that kept him from finding his pot of gold.

He knew what he did not want:

- To pay transaction fees for every check that needed to be executed
- To wait for his custodian's permission or review of "deal" which only causes delays and keeps him from lucrative investments
- To pay asset charges on the value of his portfolio which only helps boost his custodian bank account

He may find the answer in the ultimate 21st century investment tool: the Self-Directed IRA LLC!

√ Summary Check List

- You don't have to be wealthy to become a self-directed IRA investor.
- Self-directed IRA investing is a proven investment concept.
- Ask yourself the eight questions to determine if your IRA is a genuine self-directed IRA.
- Three key providers are necessary: a custodian or administer and the self-directed IRA Advisor

"I know of no more encouraging fact than the unquestioned ability of a man to elevate his life by conscious endeavor"

Henry David Thoreau

"Think like a man of action, act like a man of thought"

Henri Bergson

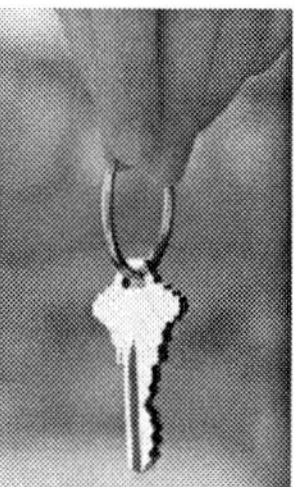

SELF-DIRECTED IRA LLC

The LLC (Limited Liability Corporation) is the ultimate 21st Century investing tool. It's half way between a corporation and a partnership and gives you the liability protection of a corporation, which means the IRA member is not liable for the LLC.

IN THE DRIVER'S SEAT

Raymond heaves a sigh of relief when he finally completes his research on an IRA LLC, and understood the spirit underlying its mechanics. He has finally discovered a legal entity that would truly allow him to manage his IRA his own way. He would be in the driver's seat not only in name but also in deed. His IRA would be a member of the LLC; he could direct the profits from his LLC to his IRA, and these profits would be tax-free.

▶ **Note**: He owes no taxes unless he elects a distribution from the plan.

THE IRA LLC MECHANICS

We advised Raymond he could buy an IRA LLC either with his Traditional or Roth IRA.

Since his IRA would be a member of the LLC, or own a share in it, the IRA funds could legally be transferred to the LLC in exchange for member units (shares) of the LLC. He could then purchase investments through the LLC, and directly control them.

In the end, the value of the LLC will flow back to his IRA as part of his normal IRA retirement amount. Through the IRA LLC he will truly witness the power of non-traditional investments unleashed in the self-directed way.

▶ **Note**: The profits from the investment are gains not contribution. Contributions are funds you place into the IRA.

Raymond and His IRA LLC

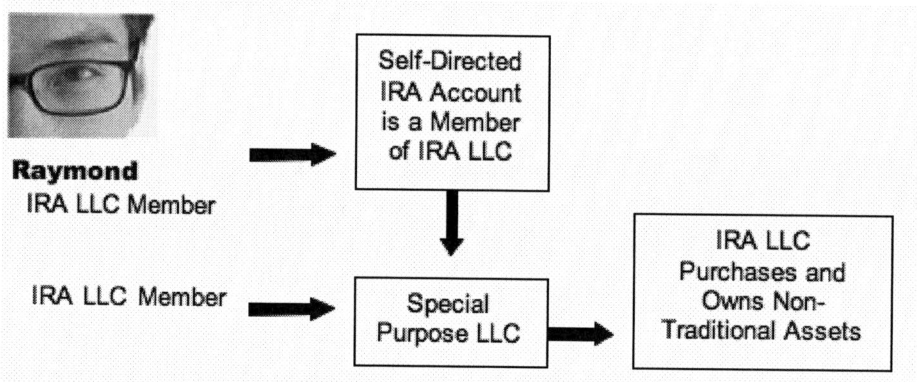

▶ **Note**: The language in the operating agreement is compliant to the IRS code unlike normal operating agreements used for business purposes. The filing is also different again, not the same as a business entity would be filed.

Energy Sources From the IRA LLC

Being in the driver's seat" is a great concept and music to Raymond's ears. However, he needs to know whether it would last, whether like froth and bubble it would disappear, or whether it was connected to lasting energy sources. There is good news on this front! The LLC is powerful because it draws its power from long-term energy sources that also generate immense benefits to the investor.

Checkbook Control

The LLC lets Raymond write checks. He can decide where, when and how much to invest within a timeframe of his choosing. Other investors had explained earlier the perils of costly delays. He heard examples of the IRA custodian not supporting a choice of investment. For example: Darin Davis' frustrating experience.

"There were two or three times I was unable to make any investments as fast as I needed to, that were very profitable investments and I saw them make money for other people and I was unable to participate because I could not get to my money fast enough. So that's what drove me to the LLC." Darin Davis, CEO, Captuity Investments Firm, Inc.

Asset Protection

People die, people get divorced, and the situation changes financially. We live in a very litigious society so you need the extra asset protection you have through your IRA LLC. The worst that can happen with the LLC is that you lose the money that's in the deal itself; you don't lose the whole IRA.

Raymond has also researched the asset protection attributes of an LLC and found them quite powerful.

By isolating his investment inside the IRA LLC and away from the rest of his IRA funds and his estate, Raymond can substantially reduce litigation threats associated with investments such as real estate.

Henry Novak, an experienced attorney shared a useful example during a seminar:

"If you put a six unit apartment complex into an LLC, and a gas explosion occurs due to your oversight of repairs that should have been done but weren't, your LLC may be sued, but not you personally. If the judgment goes against you, they could foreclose on the property and sell it off, taking the equity to satisfy the judgment, but they couldn't get to you.

However, if you owned that property personally and it was not in an LLC, they could take whatever they could get from you."

Another form of asset protection comes from having one or more partners in the LLC. Upon applying the above example to an LLC with multiple partners Raymond realized that whatever judgment is delivered would impact only his share of the income stream, not the entire property.

Investment Authority

With checkbook control, Raymond is able to make his own investment decisions unfettered by custodian-driven restrictions and approval. Furthermore, there isn't a need to pay a fee to the custodian for review.

Low Flat Custodial Fee

Since all Raymond's IRA assets would be placed into one super asset, an LLC, his custodian would have only one asset to manage, resulting in an inexpensive flat custodial fee.

"If you give people the freedom to create a retirement system, they are able to make their own decisions. Instead of paying someone else a commission to buy or sell stock, you do it yourself. Being able to have checkbook control over one's retirement is peace of mind." Philip King and Jeanine King, Owners, Lowell King Insurance Service

Final Kick Off

Raymond has researched, read, heard, and talked about the merits of an IRA LLC and he's ready for the final kick off to realize its advantages:

You can diversify - Unlike stand-alone IRA accounts an IRA LLC lets you diversify your investments speedily, conveniently, and safely.

You defer capital gains - When you sell real estate or other investments through your IRA LLC, capital gains are deferred through your IRA, like any other IRA investment. You do not have to deal with the headaches of 1031exchanges.

You are in Tax Heaven - You enjoy a tremendous built-in tax advantage. LLC's are taxed as a partnership, which means taxes are paid by the member of the LLC, who in your case is your IRA. Since your IRA is tax exempt, your investment is effectively tax-free.

You can use IRA LLC funds as Down Payment - As the owner of your IRA LLC, you can use your LLC funds as a down payment for a real estate purchase - residential or commercial. However your IRA cannot directly guarantee such a financing arrangement.

IS THE IRA LLC FOR ONE AND ALL?

An IRA LLC is not the magic pill for everyone's investment woes; Raymond needs to understand that setting up an LLC would not be advisable if:

- He believes that he might be tempted to use his funds for non-investment purposes;
- He has insufficient investing experience or did not have a self-directed IRA advisor to work with;
- He is the type of investor waiting for the IRS to proclaim its approval of an IRA LLC. He would be waiting in vain because that proclamation might never occur. Case in point, nowhere in the IRS code is it stated that a mutual fund is an "approved investment" for an IRA.

How should Raymond start the buying process?

Raymond has several choices:

- He can transfer or roll over all or part of his funds to a self-directed IRA;
- He can open an IRA LLC as a tax advantaged vehicle; or
- He can choose to own the LLC in its entirety or purchase units with other partners. Both have advantages. With the latter, profits are equally distributed, business risks are shared, and investment choices increase.

Raymond is excited about purchasing an IRA LLC, but he should know that even though buying an IRA LLC would place him in the driver's seat, he needs a self-directed IRA advisor to help him maneuver his retirement money through the correct gateways.

√ Summary Check List

- IRA LLC provides you checkbook control, asset protection, investment authority, and a low flat custodial fee.
- As the owner of your IRA LLC, you can use your LLC funds as a down payment for a real estate purchase.
- Since your IRA is tax exempt, your investment is effectively tax-free until distribution.
    - The Roth is truly tax-free

Plans fail for lack of counsel, but with many advisers they succeed.

NIV Proverbs 15:22

"In the end, all business operations can be reduced to three words; people, product and profits. Unless you've got a good team, you can't do much with the other two"

Lee Iacocca

THE SELF-DIRECTED IRA ADVISOR

A self-directed IRA provides you freedom, but you need an advisor to keep you grounded. You still have to play within the rules.

HOW A SELF-DIRECTED IRA ADVISOR CAN HELP RAYMOND

Tracking Legal and Administrative Issues

A self-directed IRA has various legal and administrative components. Raymond needs help keeping track of them, and processing them in the right order. A self-directed IRA advisor can help corral these pieces, giving Raymond more time to focus on investment choices.

Providing the Scoop on Non-traditional Investments

A self-directed IRA advisor always knows "what's new" on the non-traditional investments front. Raymond would always have the scoop on the inside story. This would help him stay one step ahead of the game. Without a self-directed IRA advisor, John would be treading on thin ice.

Setting up the IRA LLC

Setting up an IRA LLC involves many procedures and requires compliance on various fronts. A self-directed IRA advisor helps take care of most of these. The advisor also ensures that the LLC has asset protection in place to protect Raymond from creditors, predators and litigation.

Warnings of Potential Legal Pitfalls

(Rather than Micro managing Investments)

The self-directed IRA advisor would be the one on red alert ensuring that Raymond's investments did not violate prohibited transaction rules or other IRS provisions. e.g., per IRS rules, real estate purchased with an IRA cannot be used for personal benefit.

Strong Support

A credible and reputable self-directed IRA advisor will follow through on every task and provide support with every procedure. Some advisors only promote offers without providing ongoing support or customer care. They might say you'll need to have your attorney provide an opinion letter or they'll provide you with a few hours of representation when you go to court.

We cautioned Raymond to remember the following when selecting a Self-Directed IRA advisor:

- Verify the advisor's credentials with the Better Business Bureau and the advisor's state Attorney General's office.
- Ensure that the advisor complies with state licensing requirements.
- Check that the advisor is certified.

Raymond feels assured that selecting a self-directed IRA advisor is the next milestone on his journey. He wants to know a little more about the Asset Exchange Group before signing on.

√ Summary Check List

- You need an experienced self-directed Advisor to help and support you.
- Select a self-directed IRA Advisor by:
    - Verifying the Advisor's credentials
    - Ensuring that the Advisor complies with state licensing requirements
    - Checking that the Advisor is certified

"Before anything else, preparation is the key to success"

Alexander Graham Bell

"Yesterday I dared to struggle. Today I dare to win"

Bernadette Devlin

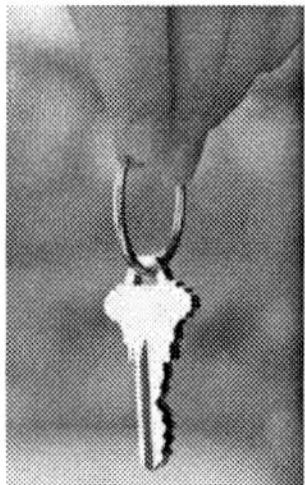

AEG SOLUTIONS

AEG's customized IRA LLC structure and ongoing follow-up and support keep client investments compliant with IRS rules and away from prohibited transactions.

Wall Street Savvy and Top-Notch Support on Main Street

When we first met Raymond he had said, *"I have had success investing in real estate and want to be able to use my IRA for real estate."* The structure that we had to offer is in harmony with his goals.

As Raymond further explores the benefits of the AEG path, he notes that everyone who calls on AEG receives something significant: clarification, advice, resources, referrals, out-of-the box ideas, encouragement, and ongoing customer support.

We proudly tell Raymond that the feather in our cap is the customized structure that we provide for each client's IRA LLC. This structure and ongoing follow up will keep Raymond's investments compliant with IRS rules and away from prohibited transactions.

SPECIALIZED SERVICES

Customized Structure

Unlike other players in the IRA market, we walk our clients through the process and beyond: Raymond will not be on his own because AEG gives him the operating guide, and consult with an AEG advisor gives him the warranty he is seeking and clears all his doubts.
As Philip King and Jeanine King, Owners, Lowell King Insurance Service describes, "AEG is always willing to answer our questions. They always returned our phone calls and walked us through the IRA LLC process. We've relied on their knowledge and research. They are top notch. They have come through for us when we have had questions concerning our decision."

Innovative Advice

Raymond will enjoy the informal approach that a smaller company provides instead of spending time interpreting a big company's procedures. With AEG's direction, he can do it himself.

The AEG innovative approach helps Raymond realize his goals faster. We educate clients on the whole gamut of investment options, something that other IRA trustees need not do. Other IRA trustees are permitted to impose additional restrictions on investments. Because of administrative burdens, many of them do not permit IRA owners to invest IRA funds in real estate. Even though the IRS does not prohibit real estate investments, trustees are not required to offer real estate as an option.

We assist our clients in identifying any prohibited transactions, which are likely to result in a penalty or taxes, or even lead to the IRA being disqualified.

"People are stunned when they learn about the scope of what is possible with a self-directed IRA account and an IRA LLC, even those who think they know all about IRAs. You need a sophisticated advisor who understands the legal issues and guides you through the process. I can thank Asset Exchange Group for helping me." John, former senior executive in a Fortune 250 company, and current owner of a manufacturing company

Don't get left high and dry after a deal. You need information on what to do next. AEG answers questions like these: How do I file my taxes? I don't know if I can do this with my IRA or, are we supposed to put this in the compliance review?

Empowering Processes

We emphasize to Raymond that he is in the driver's seat because of his investment choices and AEG's processes that include:

- Assessing his unique objectives, risk tolerance, and other personal factors, such as family circumstances, employment status, and other socio-economic criteria that might influence his investment decisions.

- Presenting him various options on positioning his genuine self-directed IRA portfolio so he can minimize risk and maximize returns on his investment.
- Helping reduce his investment risks and liability by setting up a genuine self-directed IRA LLC.
- Ensuring that his IRA LLC is drafted in compliance with all IRS and Department of Labor (DOL) rules. An improperly drafted IRA may be disqualified and taxed.
- Offering him a wide array of investment choices.
- Analyzing whether a specific investment deal is right for him.
- Interpreting the attorney's legal operating guide with him.
- Implementing the steps of the IRA LLC purchase process.
- Providing continuing support after his IRA LLC purchase.

Comprehensive Services Package

Slowly but surely Raymond can see how AEG helps clients before, during and after a transaction. AEG;

- Uses their expertise in industry regulations to lower fees, and cut administration overhead;
- Has tax attorneys on staff who provide accurate informaton and flexible tools to help ensure that investments comply with IRS rules; and

- Customizes their customer support by teaching their clients how to set up, use, and capitalize on their IRA LLC's.

If Raymond is successful in his first deal, with AEG support he can walk confidently into the next one.

"I am always pushing the envelope, trying to find out how I can make more money, have more money in leverage and opportunity, and if I get to something I'm not a 100% sure of, I have access to AEG.
I go in and actually give them the scenario, give them the legalities, and get their feedback as to what I can or cannot do." Darin Davis, CEO, Captuity Investments, Inc.

√ Summary Check List:

- You can invest in assets as diverse as homes, horses, and bridge loans.
- Knowing your options is key: remember, even though the IRS does not prohibit real estate investments, trustees are not required to offer real estate as an option.

THE AEG PROCESS

Asset Exchange Group works with investors to assess their unique objectives, risk tolerance and other factors, educate them on options and institute a program that allows them to select from a much greater breadth of investment choices.

Raymond has completed his due diligence process. He is now even more confident that a genuine self-directed IRA and an IRA LLC are the structures he needs to maximize his retirement funds.

We inform Raymond of the various steps, and the numerous actions AEG takes when setting up a genuine self-directed IRA and an IRA LLC. Our process is the key to Raymond's successful self-directed investing!

PROCESS FLOW CHART

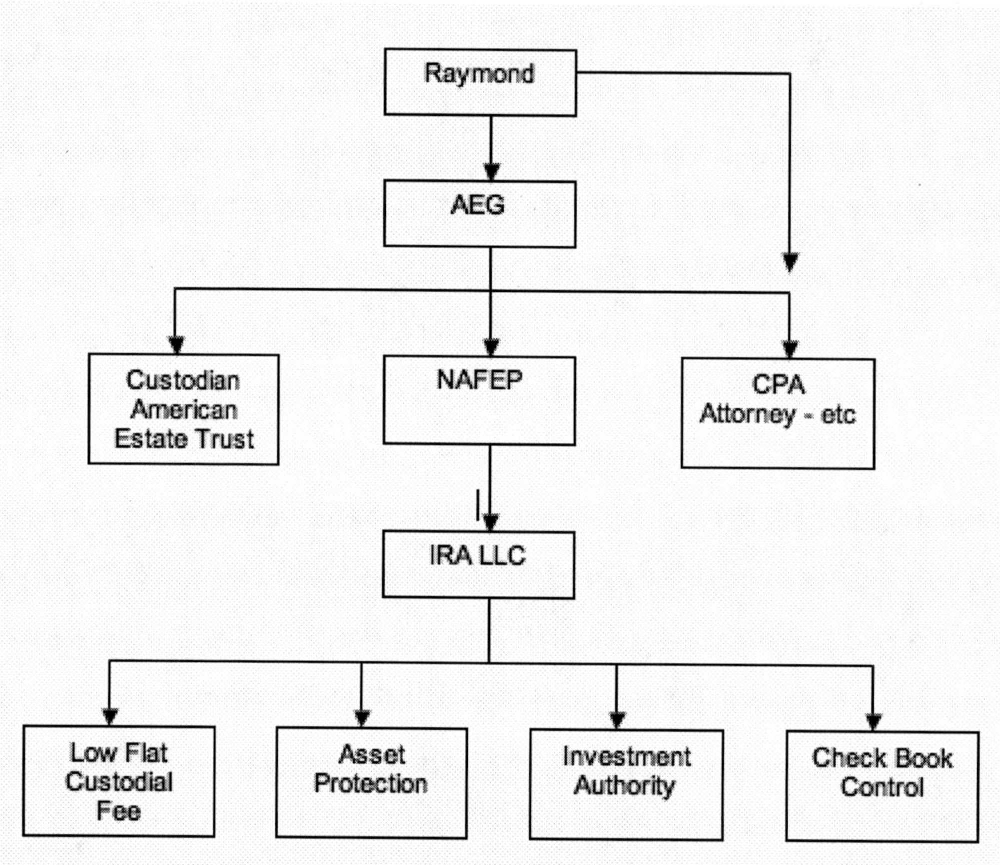

AEG Procedures

Player	Customized Actions
AEG Advisor	**Assesses** your goals, and informs you about investment options. Obtains from you details concerning the amount of money you are willing and able to invest - minimum of $25,000 is recommended. **Asks** how you'd like your IRA LLC to be structured. For example, you might want to use your IRA, or include your spouse's funds or spouse's IRA. **Recommends** that you open a genuine self-directed IRA with a self-directed IRA custodian like American Estate Trust. **If you** do not need checkbook control, AEG directs you to www.trusteeamerica.com
American Estate Trust	**Arranges** a transfer of your funds from your current custodian to American Estate Trust. If your money is in a Roth IRA, arranges a transfer of funds to another Roth IRA with a new plan document that allows funds to be used for non-traditional investments.
AEG	**Helps** you complete a National Association of Financial Estate Planners (NAFEP) application, a pre-requisite for ordering an IRA LLC document package from NAFEP. **Completes** the necessary state filings.
NAFEP	**Completes** the LLC legal document package, using a patented operating agreement - Premier IV ICO™. You can operate as

	the manager of your LLC.
AEG	**Sets up** an LLC that is 100% compliant with IRS provisions (IRS 4975). **Applies** for your LLC employer identification number (EIN). **Arranges** for your IRA funds to be transferred to your LLC. **Trains** you to operate the LLC. **Helps** you fund a checking account at a local bank so you can begin investing with your LLC. **Instructs** your custodian to place your IRA assets into the LLC bank account.
American Estate Trust	**Reports** applicable fund transfers and balances to the IRS. As your custodian, American Estate Trust is also responsible for making distributions to you. **Transfers** money to the LLC in the form of purchasing membership units in the LLC.
AEG and NAFEP	**Collaborate** to procure for you non-traditional investment assets, such as real estate, notes, liens, private stock. You can begin investing from the LLC.
AEG	**Refers** you to an investment advisor, if needed. **Continues** to provide follow-up customer care by keeping you informed of regulations, procedures, and government actions.

Raymond is now ready to complete his money story. He believes that his financial chasm days are behind him, and he can now walk with confidence across the bridge to the non-traditional investments side.

He knows he will live to tell the tale and recruit other chasm dwellers to make the successful journey with him.

√ Summary Check List

- AEG's group of experienced professionals set industry standards.
- AEG's procedures are customized to the needs of each client.

"According to legend, one day a man was wandering in the desert when he met Fear and Plague. They said they were on their way to a large city where they were going to kill 10,000 people. The man asked Plague if he was going to do all the work. Plague smiled and said, "No, I'll only take care of a few hundred. I'll let my friend Fear do the rest"

Anon

PILLOW TALK WITH THE IRS

Raymond gets the *jitters.* He has just become the target of one of the most successful marketing campaigns known to mankind – the IRS-driven, fear-based campaign! We'll refer to this as
"pillow talk".

Raymond's journey is almost complete and he is ready for a rest. Wham! Instead of peaceful slumber, an intrusive mental video begins playing, rewinding, and playing again. This is not just an annoying advertising jingle, but a sound track bearing grim warnings about the IRS, forebodings of unsafe investments, and pronouncements of potential financial disaster.

Various questions plagued Raymond. Should he join the ranks of those who are afraid of potentially running afoul of the IRS and its perceived ability to ruin lives? Is his decision to pursue a genuine self-directed IRA and an IRA LLC worth all the potential aggravation? With AEG help he examines his pillow talk and scrutinizes facts that challenge it.

We hope Raymond realizes that most of his pillow talk jitters is triggered by ignorance.

Pillow Talk Jitters and Facts

Jitters: The IRS might not approve of assets such as real estate, tax liens or notes.

Fact: The IRS administers and enforces internal revenue laws; it does not review or approve investments. Refer to "An Important Message For Tax Payers". For example, mutual funds are not an "approved" investment, and yet are the largest retirement funds asset purchased in retirement accounts.

Jitters: Both my accountant and financial advisor say investing in non-traditional assets is risky, and I may lose everything if I am audited.

Fact: In defense of your accountant, the IRS library has over 45,000 pages of code. Knowing it all is impossible. Your accountant and/or advisor are most likely confident about what they know or have been taught. They are possibly familiar with some compliance rules.

But anything beyond their knowledge horizon will seem "risky"! Do they want to continue managing your assets? Probably yes! So driving you away with their fears is not in their best interests.

Jitters: All this talk of genuine self-directed IRAs is cutting edge. But I wonder if it is legal? Black suited agents might be lurking in the woods, battering ram in hand, ready to storm my home!

Fact: Actually, this self-directed IRA process has been around since 1974. Those who wanted to have their IRAs genuinely self-directed sought and obtained the means to get it done. After the market crash of 2000 and widespread Internet research, many people turned toward this profitable method of growing their retirement funds.

"The most exciting aspect of my self-directed investments is the ability to get in and out of investments, while complying with IRS guidelines at the same time" John, former senior executive in a Fortune 250 company and current owner of a manufacturing company.

"I don't have any regrets about my self-directed IRA investment decisions; I just wish we had started earlier" Philip King and Jeanine King, Owners of Lowell King Insurance Service.

Jitters: This is too good to be true. What if my retirement, especially my Roth IRA, makes a lot of money? It might raise a red flag with the black-suited IRS agents!

Fact: No they are not concerned at all. Remember all the dot-com stocks that went from $5.00 to $300? Was anyone concerned at the time that retirement accounts gained huge multiples? Not at all!

Jitters: I still break into a sweat when I think of the "checkbook control" I'd have with an IRA LLC. Didn't an attorney write somewhere that there is no substantiating proof that you can write checks against your IRA funds?

Fact: Well this attorney probably just did not do enough research. Besides, since bad and alarming news sells fast, why should editors worry about being fair and balanced? Don't forget that they continually press their perspective regardless of the facts.

Refer to Section 4975 of the IRS tax code for information regarding self-dealing.

Mr. Swanson Turned the Tide

We suggest to Raymond that it is time to hit the "Stop" button and look at someone who effectively turned the tide in favor of using a self-directed IRA effectively. The person was Mr. Swanson, and his actions are described in the Tax Court opinion (Swanson v. Commissioner, 106 TC 76106 TC No. 3, 1996).

Mr. Swanson, a taxpayer, upon advice of legal counsel:

1. Opened a new self-directed IRA.

2. Formed Foreign Service Corporation (FSC) similar to an IRA LLC.
3. Named himself director, and then later president of the corporation.
4. Directed the IRA custodian to purchase shares of the corporation (the IRA was the only shareholder).
5. As president of the corporation, directed (with custodian consent) that the corporation pay its dividends to the IRA.

The corporation acted as a commissioned sales agent for a manufacturing company, which Mr. Swanson also owned. So income, which would normally be taxed to the manufacturing corporation, was instead funneled to the corporation as sales commissions.

The court held that the corporation was a "domestic international sales corporation" (DISC) under section 991 of the tax code, and not subject to income tax, except for the taxes imposed by chapter 5 of the IRS tax code. So the gross income was paid out on a tax deferred basis to Mr. Swanson's IRA.

Mr. Swanson also handled the sales for the corporation because it had no employees. Since he took no wages or salary, the entire corporation's income flowed tax-deferred to the IRA. Neither the IRS nor the Tax Court challenged this aspect of the Swanson arrangement.

IRS Response

The IRS:

1. Audited Mr. Swanson's transaction,
2. Initially held that the transaction violated the prohibited transaction rules of section 4975 of the tax code, and
3. After protracted wrangling, agreed that the entire IRA LLC-type transaction is in fact legal.

Mr. Swanson's Dual Victory

Mr. Swanson incurred significant legal expenses in battling the IRS over a position, which they, in effect, agreed was wrong.

He demanded that the IRS pay his legal fees. The IRS refused. So he pursued his claim in Tax Court.

The Tax Court concluded that:

- Mr. Swanson's IRA LLC-type arrangement was not illegal; and
- The IRS had to reimburse Mr. Swanson a reasonable amount of his legal fees.

▶ **Note:** Refer to details of the Tax Court statement in the NAFEP research memo.

Mr. Swanson won two victories

The IRS compensated him as well as covered his legal costs. This is crucial since the IRS usually goes to court only when it thinks it can win, and if it does lose, it rarely pays anything on the way out.

The IRS issued a memo to its revenue agents announcing that the structure form of the IRA LLC is not a prohibited transaction.

Another Positive IRS Response

In 2001, the senior technical reviewer of the Office of the Chief Counsel of the IRS wrote a field service advisory (FSA) memo (FSA 200128011) to the IRS counsel at a regional branch, considering whether or not to challenge an IRA LLC-type arrangement similar to Mr. Swanson's.

In this case the IRA LLC entity was owned by four separate IRAs; related parties, father and his three children. In the light of the Swanson case, however, the IRS decided not to challenge the IRA LLC-type arrangement.

Other Challengers to Pillow Talk

Pass Through Tax Entity

An LLC is a pass through tax entity and can be managed by the IRA owner. Without employees the LLC would be ignored for tax purposes. The Department of Labor (DOL) has regularly viewed IRA LLC-type arrangements as legal under federal tax law.

DOL opinion is binding on the IRS with regard to pension and retirement plans, including IRAs. A significant example is Advisory Opinion 2000-10A, where the physical arrangement that DOL approved was a partnership instead of a limited liability company. In this case, Mr. Adler, the IRA owner, also owned a 6.5 percent interest in the partnership.

Since both the LLC and partnerships are pass through entities there is no material difference between them for purposes of an LLC discussion. In fact, if an LLC has more than one owner (member), it is treated as a partnership under tax law.

The DOL, the IRS, and the Tax Court have all issued definitive statements, rulings and opinions in the favor of owning non-traditional assets in an IRA. This proves to Raymond that this LLC concept is not aggressive, risky, or even new.

Health Savings Accounts (HSA) and Checkbook Control

Health Savings Accounts are built upon the same IRS code as the IRA.

In fact, at age 65 you have a choice of continuing to maintain your account as an HSA or converting it to an IRA. Consider this – many custodians offer the HSA holder a Check Card to pay for medical purchases or services. Is this not the same as checkbook control offered by an IRA LLC?

The IRS has not proclaimed that the checkbook is legal as a reasonable way of managing expenses.

The one difference between an HSA and any other IRA is that the HSA holder may be required to submit receipts to the custodian. But for the most part the HSA holder is on the honor system.

The intrusive mental video finally stops playing, and Raymond slips into sound slumber content that he has made the right choice!

√ Summary Check List

- Facts will overcome any uncertainties you may have about self-directed investing.
- The IRS states the structure form of the IRA LLC is not a prohibited transaction.

"A journey is a person in itself; no two are alike. And all plans, safeguards, policing, and coercion are fruitless. We find that after years of struggle that we do not take a trip; a trip takes us"

John Steinbeck

" Spectacular achievement is always preceded by unspectacular preparation"

Robert Schuller

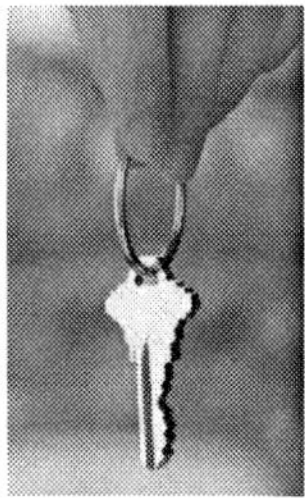

OTHER SIDE OF THE BRIDGE

It is now up to you to supercharge your portfolios by intelligently looking at alternative investments and working with an advisor that meets your needs.

Pot of Gold!

Raymond is successfully journeying towards completing his money story. His pot of gold is close at hand. As he crosses from traditional to non-traditional investments, he goes through twists and turns, and typical transition phases. He is not alone in this. Other investors on the same path experience these too.

He reflects on what it is that keeps him going towards his pot of gold: sound knowledge, due diligence, and successful investor experiences help immensely. But it is something within himself that keeps him going. During each transition phase he tackles his fears, embraces new experiences, accepts and uses AEG support, and gathers sufficient momentum to journey further.

Raymond decides to retrace his self-talk, responses and actions during each transition phase.

▶"You manage my money. I trust you more than me"

Here's where Raymond depended on his custodian and advisor (e.g. Fidelity, Charles Schwab, or Merrill Lynch) to manage and invest his IRA funds in traditional investments, e.g. stocks, bonds or mutual funds depending on:
How quickly he wanted to see his income appreciate, and
How much of an investment risk he was willing to take.

▶ "It's okay, I'll manage my investments myself"

During this phase Raymond was at a higher level of investment knowledge and confidence, and better understood his risk tolerance level and investment objectives. He still retained his money with Fidelity, Charles Schwab, or Merrill Lynch; however, they gave him the freedom to decide where to invest as long as it is within their range of traditional products like stocks, bonds, and mutual funds.

▶"I stare at a chasm"

In this phase, Raymond became aware that somewhere out there were many productive investment opportunities that were non-securities related. After some exploration and research, it dawned on him that he could invest his IRA funds in these non-traditional assets. However, frustration seeped in when he realized that he did not fully grasp the processes and procedures involved with non-traditional investments."

▶"I see the bridge but encounter obstacles on the way"

Raymond learned about a different kind of provider called a self-directed IRA custodian (e.g., American Estate Trust) who allowed him the freedom to invest in non-traditional assets. He decided to cross a portion of the bridge and began enjoying newfound opportunities, but soon encountered obstacles:

He needed permission for every single deal. He may or may not have received this permission in a timely manner.

He had to pay an asset fee based on the asset's value. As an IRA holder, if he worked hard to build his portfolio, the custodian would win. But if he lost, the custodian lost nothing.

He was at the custodian's mercy to obtain checks on a timely and accurate basis, often having to pay prohibitive delivery charges.
His custodian would not be liable if faulty delivery caused the check to be inadvertently cashed by the wrong person.

▶"I can cross the bridge with a little help"
Raymond was introduced to the IRA LLC as a viable option and realized that this was the answer to all his transition hurdles. He received a complete package from a genuine self-directed advisor who:

- Advised him on how practical it was for him to purchase an IRA LLC.

- Facilitated his funds transfer from his traditional to non-traditional custodian.
- Helped him purchase the IRA LLC.
- Informed him of the feasibility of each of his new ventures from an IRS perspective.

▶"I am in control"

After purchasing an IRA LLC, Raymond was in the driver's seat of his financial destiny and had no one but himself to credit or blame for the results of his investments. He knew he was in command of his investments when:

- He could gauge his achievements in a year.
- He completed a transaction and his IRA LLC profited.
- He successfully and efficiently initiated and completed several deals.

Raymond knows that he may encounter other transition issues but is confident that his knowledge, experience, and AEG support will help him to successfully deal with them too.

WHAT'S IN YOUR POT OF GOLD?

Raymond is now a happy camper. The chaos on Wall Street doesn't bother him anymore. His IRA LLC has helped bring his money story to a successful finish. He has begun investing his IRA funds in real estate and is exploring other investment possibilities.

The most important thing to be aware of is that an IRA LLC is not one of several similar cookies in a cookie jar. You cannot buy it off the shelf; you've got to travel towards it using a process that is customized for you. And on the journey you'll encounter your own opportunities, which will finally lead you to your very own pot of gold – just as these other happy campers have:

"We bought 240 acres in a tree farm. We believe the value of this property will go up three times in five years" Philip King and Jeanine King, Owners of Lowell King Insurance Service.

"Eighteen months later I had an equity position so that when the developer sold that property the $55,000 capital came back to my IRA plus $83,000 of profit" Darin Davis, CEO, Captuity Investments, Inc.

"I buy single family homes in Austin and surrounding areas. I buy undervalued homes, turn them around and resell them, or rent them" Mike Springer, Agent at Global Realty Marketing.

"I am planning to invest in ocean front property in Belize which apparently is structured for Self-Directed IRA's" John, Current Owner, Manufacturing Company

Philip and Jeanine, Darin, Mike, John, and Raymond are a few people who are discovering their own pot of gold. What you discover in your pot of gold depends on the quality of your journey. You may clutch the bridge railings in terror and close your eyes to the opportunities.

Or you may decide to bungee jump along the way and embrace opportunities too quickly. Or you may choose to embrace the risks in your path or let them overwhelm you. Or you may seek a self-directed IRA LLC, and walk the bridge slowly but surely.

√ Summary Check List

- Your self-directed Advisor helps you transition from traditional investing to the IRA LLC self-directed method.
- A self-directed IRA LLC provides you freedom to choose your investment
- Whereas, traditional investment companies give you the freedom to invest only in the products they provide.

"I don't want to get to the end of my life and find that I lived just the length of it. I want to have lived the width of it as well"

Diane Ackerman

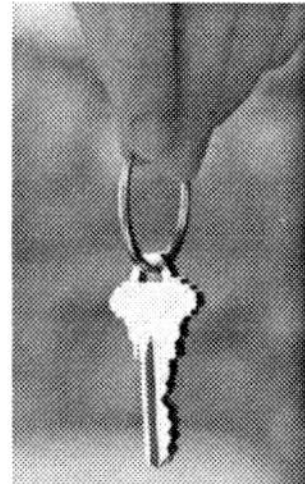

HOW TO CONDUCT A MEANINGFUL DUE-DILIGENCE INVESTIGATION

You are investigating the possibility of a self-directed IRA being the right choice for you. An IRA LLC has become a possible solution for your retirement goals, however you are unsure of tax code issues and/or what questions to ask to satisfy those questions before going forward.

THE PROCESS OF DUE-DILIGENCE

This is very important and should be conducted with utmost care. The following process will help you get on track and determine if this is the right program for you.

PHASE 1: DECISION TO INVESTIGATE

Process Activities & Milestones	Outcome & Goals	Client To-Do List & Resource List	Completion Status & Next Steps
You have decided to investigate the possibility of owning an IRA LLC. You've received product and services information. You are ready to start the investigation process.	Understand components needed for successful Due-Diligence.	Actual IRS Codes Court cases regarding IRA LLC's Professional tax and legal counsel.	Identify material. Identify counsel.

PHASE 2: THE IRS CODE

Process Activities & Milestones	Outcome & Goals	Client To-Do List & Resource List	Completion Status & Next Steps
What codes cover IRA's? What are the prohibitions? Why am I getting conflicting information from custodians?	You understand what codes to review and who to approach for help.	IRS Code 408 covers IRA's. IRS Section 4975 covers prohibited transactions and parties. Who do I ask for help?	Armed with questions, where do I go for confirmation and advice?

PHASE 3: PROFESSIONAL GUIDANCE

Process Activities & Milestones	Outcome & Goals	Client To-Do List & Resource List	Completion Status & Next Steps
What to ask your CPA. The problem with Uncle Bob.	Correct sources used and appropriate questions asked.	Your CPA has reviewed code, asked for clarification of unclear areas: asked correct questions. Professional staff conferred with each other. Example: AEG tax attorneys clarify codes with your CPA.	Complete Due-Diligence on AEG.

PHASE 4: AEG DUE-DILIGENCE PROCESS

Process Activities & Milestones	Outcome & Goals	Client To-Do List & Resource List	Completion Status & Next Steps
Who is AEG? What are their qualifications? Staff qualifications? How are they different from the competition?	Asset Exchange Group, LLC is determined to be "the" advisory group to use.	Review qualification material. Review competitive information.	Ready to make decision.

PHASE 5: DUE-DILIGENCE PROCESS COMPLETED

Process Activities & Milestones	Outcome & Goals	Client To-Do List & Resource List	Completion Status & Next Steps
Correct resources have been referenced. Appropriate questions have been asked. Decision made whether or not to proceed.	Make decision to go forward or gather final data.	Review of Due-Diligence results with AEG for any clarifications or remaining questions.	Decision made.

Uncle Bob

Uncle Bob (perhaps a close or distant relative of yours) is our toughest competitor. We have not had the privilege of building a solid relationship with you. But there is one factor that works in OUR favor: our tax attorneys on staff have examined the tax code with a fine-toothed comb to determine that our concept is VALID AND SOUND.

WHEN CUSTODIANS GIVE CONFLICTING ANSWERS

1. If you have complete control of your IRA, a custodian cannot charge you transaction fees.

2. The person you're talking to at Custodian X only knows what he has been taught. He does not and should not interpret tax laws.

3. Ask him why an IRA is prohibited from owning an LLC. Ask him to name the particular provision in the code that states this explicitly.

4. Ask him about his professional background. A recent graduate? What training other than the custodial classes has he had specifically in retirement planning? What training or investigation does he have relating to tax codes?
5. Chances are that his answers are mere policies that sound like tax codes. Satisfy yourself by asking him if investing in real estate overseas is allowed.

6. Make it clear to him that you are working with Asset Exchange Strategies. He may modify his position.

DO YOU NEED IRS PERMISSION?

The answer is no. The tax codes are written with very few permission clauses. If the code does not prohibit the transaction, then it is permissible as long as it does not conflict with the current codes.

For example, there is no code that states that the purchase of securities or insurance related products (annuities) using your retirement funds are permitted. But the question of whether or not real estate is permitted is still asked.

WHAT TO ASK THE PROFESSIONAL ADVISOR

We strongly encourage you to seek professional guidance and advice. Hopefully, you have benefitted from good counsel in the past and will continue to do so in the future. When you speak to your Advisor ask the following questions:

Did you read the code?

We find that some Advisors have not read the code thoroughly because it is new to them and therefore they shy away from the details, details that matter. It seems always safer not to rock the boat rather than scrutinize it.

What is a prohibited transaction?

Is our proposal a prohibited transaction? If Advisors are unable to substantiate a prohibited transaction, why should there be grounds for concern? Gut feeling or smell test is NOT solid advice.

Did you read the court ruling Swanson vs. the IRS?

This was a very compelling case that highlighted the taxpayer's ability to have the same control over his IRA.

What was the significance of the Court judging the IRS allegations as "frivolous"?

It demonstrated that the IRS position had no basis in law or in fact. Because their claims were groundless, the case was dismissed!

What was the significance of the IRS being ordered to pay the court costs?

The IRS very rarely has to pay for court costs. It is one tool that they effectively use to their advantage so that it deters people from filing claims against them. The Swanson case reversed that thinking.

√ Summary Check List

- Your process of due-diligence includes five phases:
    - Investigate components for a successful due-diligence
    - List your questions on IRS Codes
    - Assess professional resources
    - Select your self-directed IRA Advisor
    - Engage

"I just filled out my income tax forms. Who says you can't get killed by a blank?"

Milton Berle

THE NATIONAL ASSOCIATION FINANCIAL ESTATE PLANNING (NAFEP)

The IRA Company (ICO) Concept

ICO is the brand name NAFEP uses for the IRA LLC. Most professional advisors will find it fairly easy to accept the concept of owning non-traditional investments in an IRA. But some may have difficulty in accepting the concept of the ICO. However, the U.S. Department of Labor (DOL), the IRS and the Tax Court have all made decisive statements, rulings and opinions in the favor of this concept. The concept is not aggressive, risky or even new.

One decisive Tax Court opinion (Swanson v. Commissioner, 106 TC 76106 TC No. 3, 1996) was a case where the taxpayer, Mr. Swanson, upon advice of legal counsel opened a new, self-directed IRA, formed a new corporation, named himself as director and then later as president of the corporation. The court held that the corporation was a "domestic international sales corporation" (DISC) under section 991 of the tax code, and except for the taxes imposed by chapter 5 of the tax code, a DISC is not subject to income tax.

Swanson then directed the IRA custodian to purchase the shares of the corporation. The IRA was the only shareholder. Mr. Swanson, as president of the corporation, directed, with the custodian's consent, that the corporation pay its dividends to the IRA.

In this case, the ICO Corporation acted as a commissioned sales agent for a manufacturing company, which Mr. Swanson also owned. The effect of this arrangement was that income, which would normally be taxed to the manufacturing corporation, was instead funneled to the ICO Corporation as sales commissions. As a DISC (see above paragraph), the corporation was not a taxable entity.

The gross income was then paid out on a tax-deferred basis to the IRA of Mr. Swanson. Apparently Mr. Swanson was the person who handled the sales for the ICO Corporation, because it had no employees. And he took no wages or salary, so all or most of the corporation's income flowed tax deferred to the IRA.

Neither the IRS nor the Tax Court challenged this aspect of the Swanson arrangement.

The IRS audited this transaction and initially held that it violated the prohibited transaction rules of section 4975 of the tax code. After protracted wrangling between Swanson and the IRS, the IRS eventually agreed that the entire ICO type transaction was legal. By this time, Swanson had significant legal fees in battling the IRS over a position, which they, in effect, agreed was wrong.

Swanson then demanded payment of his legal fees, which the IRS refused. So Swanson pursued his claim for legal fees in Tax Court. Without any difficulty, the tax court reached two major conclusions: (1) Mr. Swanson's ICO type arrangement was not illegal, and (2) the IRS had to pay Swanson for a reasonable amount of his legal fees. Specifically, the Tax Court stated:

"… The dividends paid to IRA #1 were tax deferred pursuant to section 408. Thus, the net effect of these transactions was to defer recognition of dividend income that otherwise would have flowed through to any shareholders of Worldwide". (Worldwide was the ICO Corporation – NAFEP)

"At all pertinent times IRA #1 was the sole shareholder of Worldwide (the ICO corporation – NAFEP); (2) since the 2,500 shares of Worldwide issued to IRA #1 were original issue, no sale or exchange of the stock occurred; (3) from and after the dates of his appointment as director and president of Worldwide,

Mr. Swanson engaged in no activities on behalf of Worldwide which benefited him other than as a beneficiary of IRA #1; (4) IRA #1 was not maintained, sponsored, or contributed to by We find that it was unreasonable for respondent (the IRS – NAFEP) to maintain that a prohibited transaction occurred when Worldwide's stock was acquired by IRA #1. The stock acquired in that transaction was newly issued — prior to that point in time.

Worldwide had no shares or shareholders: a corporation without shares or shareholders does not fit within the definition of a disqualified person under section 4975(e)(2)(G). It was only after Worldwide issued its stock to IRA #1 that petitioner held a beneficial interest in Worldwide's stock, thereby causing Worldwide to become a disqualified person under section 4975(e)(2)(G).

Accordingly, the issuance of stock to IRA #1 did not, within the plain meaning of section 4975(c)(1)(A), qualify as a "sale or exchange, or leasing, of any property between a plan and a disqualified person". Therefore, respondent's (IRS's – NAFEP) litigation position with respect to this issue was unreasonable as a matter of both law and fact."

"Section 4975(c)(1)(E) addresses itself only to acts of disqualified persons who, as fiduciaries, deal directly or indirectly with the income or assets of a plan for their own benefit or account. Here, there was no such direct or indirect dealing with the income or assets of a plan, as the dividends paid by Worldwide did not become income of IRA #1 until unqualifiedly made subject to the demand of IRA #1. Sec. 1.301-1(b), Income Tax Regs. Furthermore, respondent has never suggested that petitioner, acting as a "fiduciary" or otherwise, ever dealt with the corpus of IRA #1 for his own benefit."

"A corporation without shares or shareholders does not fit within the definition of a disqualified person under section 4975(e)(2)(G).

Furthermore, we find that at the time of the stock issuance, Worldwide was not, within the meaning of sec. 4975(e)(2)(C), an "employer", any of whose employees were beneficiaries of IRA #1."

ACCESS TO IRA INFORMATION

The Internal Revenue Service web site is www.irs.gov. Below are a few links you may want to visit.

About Traditional	www.irs.gov/faqs/faq-kw199.html
About Roth	www.irs.gov/faqs/faq-kw156.html
SEP's	www.irs.gov/retirement/sponsor/article/0,,id=139828,00.html
SIMPLE IRA's	www.irs.gov/retirement/sponsor/article/0,,id=139831,00.html
SARSEP's	www.irs.gov/retirement/sponsor/article/0,,id=137455,00.html
Real Estate in IRA's	www.irs.gov/faqs/faq-kw88.html Why Custodians Offer Conflicting Information

"I know of no more encouraging fact than the unquestioned ability of a man to elevate his life by conscious endeavor"

Henry David Thoreau

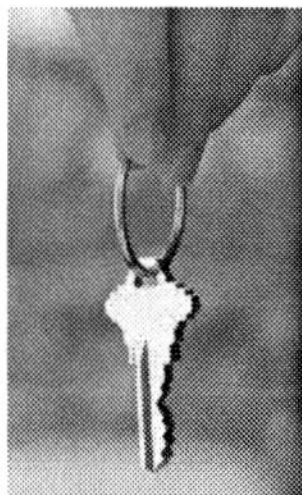

ROAD MAP TO GET STARTED

If you have made the decision to start your self-directed investing you will find this guide with tactical activities helpful. Here are the basic steps to get you started in self-directed retirement investing.

BE POSITIONED FOR SUCCESS

If you believe that the IRA LLC is a product that will benefit your retirement don't let the tail wag the dog. In other words, don't let a transaction push you to success – rather, position yourself for success. You can always have your IRA LLC invest in mutual funds while you wait for a deal to manifest.

1. Learn all you can about self-directed IRA investments. Attend an AEG self-directed investment courses in person or online

2. Set up your home office – equipment and tracking and filing system. Quicken® is generally adequate for use for accounting

3. Read the Road Map To Get Started.

4. Assemble your investment team by engaging with the AEG Advisory Group, an administrator, custodian, or trustee who provides self-directed plan services.

5. Set up a Self-Directed IRA LLC.

6. Transfer your 401(k) funds to the new IRA.

7. Begin investing: invest in real estate property; buy real estate notes, mortgages, liens and deeds, or loan short-term notes.

8. Monitor investments on a regular basis

Remember, as in any new endeavor your success will depend on your ability to analyze, negotiate, follow-through activities, organization skills, and the quality of people you decide to work with.

Goal Setting

You should define what you want to accomplish with your self-directed investing and how it will complement your retirement plan. You will succeed and thrive much faster if you can articulate your goals, and how they will be accomplished along with an action plan.

Goal: State your primary reason to start your short-term lending business.

Example: To build my initial $25,000 investment to $100,000 in gross wealth with short-term loans within three years.

Objectives: Write 3 key objectives that must be met in order for you to achieve your Goal.

Examples:

- Learn how to find, analyze, acquire, execute, and manage self-directed investment opportunities.
- Build relationships with key industry and business support contacts.
- Market my business, and initiate my first investment.

1.

2.

3.

Setting Revenue Objectives

Your Revenue Objectives: Be specific and realistic.		
1st Year $ ____________	2nd Year $ ____________	3rd Year $ ____________

EXIT STRATEGY

Be sure to have an exit strategy mapped out, specifically:

1. How to get out if the deal goes bad.
2. When to get out.

Exit strategies are best worked out based on input from your real estate, broker or other advisors.

FAQ'S

Is investing in real estate with an IRA a new concept?

No, in fact, there are more than 7 TRILLION dollars held in retirement accounts, however, only about 3% of retirement accounts are self-directed and only about 2% are invested in real estate. You have been able to invest in real estate since the day IRAs were created in the 1970s!

What is a Self-Directed IRA and how is it any different from a regular IRA?

A self-directed IRA is no different than any other IRA. Having a self-directed IRA simply means you are allowed to direct the investments of the IRA. Many custodians claim they allow you to self-direct your IRA investments, but then turn around and restrict what you can invest in. A truly self-directed IRA allows you to make the decisions without restriction.

What types of retirement accounts can be moved into Self-Directed accounts?

Traditional IRAs, SEP IRAs, Roth IRAs, 401(k)s, 403(b)s, Coverdell Education Savings (ESA) a.k.a. Educational IRAs, Qualified Annuities, Profit Sharing Plans, Money Purchase Plans, Government Eligible Deferred Compensation Plans, Keoghs

Are you an IRA Custodian?

No, but everyone with a self-directed IRA needs an administrator. Depending on your needs, we have a number of custodians that we can refer you to.

What are the differences between a self\undirected IRA and a self-directed IRA LLC?

They are both self-directed accounts. The self-directed IRA LLC is truly self-directed and you administer the account. You don't have to ask for permission to make purchases. You manage the checkbook and write checks on behalf of the IRA.

What are your fees?

$190 a year whether you have one million or a billion in your IRA.

What can I invest in if I have an IRA LLC?

Your IRA LLC can make any investment a regular LLC can as long as you stay away from insurance contracts and collectibles. Also you may not have any "self-dealings" without a DOL exemption.

Is investing in real estate in an IRA a new concept?

No. The IRS has allowed these investments for over 30 years.

Is Asset Exchange Strategies, LLC a Self-Directed IRA Custodian?

No, but everyone with a self-directed IRA needs an administrator. Depending on your needs, we have a number of custodians that we can refer you to.

What is the difference between a self-directed IRA and a self-directed IRA LLC?

They are both self-directed accounts. The self-directed IRA LLC is truly self-directed and you administer the account. You don't have to ask for permission to make purchases. You manage the checkbook and write checks on behalf of the IRA.

What are your Self-Directed IRA Custodial Fees?

$190 a year whether you have 1 million or a billion in your IRA.

What can I invest in if I have an IRA LLC?

Your IRA LLC can make any investment a regular LLC can as long as you stay away from insurance contracts and collectibles. Also you may not have any "self-dealings" without a DOL exemption.

Is self-directed IRA investing in real estate in an IRA a new concept?

No. The IRS has allowed these investments for over 30 years.

Why haven't I heard of this before? Who would tell you, your stockbroker?

They will only let you invest your IRA in investments their firm offers. At a bank you will be limited to CDs. At a brokerage firm you will be limited to stocks and bonds. As a consequence (and unfortunately for many investors) it has been a well-kept secret that they have other options for their IRAs. The traditional investment community has had control of over 97% percent of retirement accounts, and they have been making a great living off your accounts. Why would they want to let you know about alternatives that they not be able to charge for?

As investors have become more disillusioned and frustrated with traditional investment choices, they have begun looking for alternatives. After the steep stock market decline, corporate scandals and corruption (e.g. Enron, ImClone, Worldcom), many investors are seeing their retirement accounts cut in half. They are finally ready to take control of their own investments. They often want more tangible investments such as real estate, deeds of trust, gas and oil.

When they ask their current advisors and brokers, they are typically told that such investments are illegal, too complicated or that it can't be done. But those are ignorant and self-serving responses. Although the advisor's custodians and brokers may not allow it, it can be done. It is just likely you can't do it through your current custodian, so they will financially suffer if you move your money to someone who can. Rest assured, they aren't going to tell you about it.

What are the downsides of investing with a self-directed IRA?

The only downside is that some people don't want to be in charge of their own retirement investments. They are happy having someone else makes all the decisions.

A self-directed IRA is not right for them. For the rest of us who want to be involved in our retirement investments and make decisions that will affect our retirement, there are no downsides. Just be aware of the prohibited transactions / restrictions (no self-dealing). We firmly believe that you are the best steward for your money. Nobody cares as much about your retirement as you do.

Why is there so little information available on Self-Directed IRA options?

The traditional investment community has control and is making money off over 97% of the retirement accounts. Letting you to know that you have other options to the stock and bond market risks would spell/is tantamount to losing the commissions and fees they charge on your retirement accounts.

How are self-directed IRA custodians different from one other?

The government allows certain institutions to handle the accounting and reporting of IRAs. Under the law, all custodians can allow you to invest your IRA in the same types of investments (stocks, bonds, mutual funds, real estate, notes, tax liens, etc.).

However, the majority of custodians have made the decision to restrict the types of investments you can make. This is not based upon law, but it is based upon what the custodian wants to offer. However, there are a handful of custodians who allow non-traditional investments. Please contact us for a special report on self-directed custodians.

Can I invest my IRA in real estate?

Absolutely!! Currently less than 3% of retirement accounts are invested in non-traditional investments (anything other than Dow & NASDAQ stocks, bonds, CDs, etc), and less than 2% are invested in real estate, that is changing. More and more individuals are becoming more frustrated with the options offered by their current custodians. Individuals are exploring investments that they can see and touch and that have some tangible value such as real estate.

They have seen the outstanding returns that investors have historically received in real estate and want to move all or part of their retirement money into various real estate investments.

Within the broad category of real estate there are many options for investment: residential rentals, commercial properties, condominiums, manufactured homes, raw land, real estate in foreign countries, trust deeds / mortgages, and mortgage pools.

How do I know that this is legal?

This is a question that is frequently asked by investors who have never heard that they could invest in anything other than stocks and bonds in their retirement accounts. They have no idea that they can invest in real estate and many other investments. However, real estate has been an allowed investment since the day IRAs were created almost thirty years ago.

Find out for yourself by going to the Internal Revenue Service's website (www.IRS.gov). Request "Publication 590" in the search window. On pages 40-41 you will see what investments are not allowed (collectibles, life insurance, s-corporation stock, etc.). Real estate is NOT mentioned as a disallowed investment just like stocks, bonds, mutual funds are not mentioned as a disallowed investment.

Can I transfer funds from a 401K, IRA, Sep IRA, Roth IRA, or 403b and direct investments myself?

Yes. You can self-direct all of these types of accounts. They can all be invested into the Self-directed IRA LLC for truly self-directed investing.

What does the IRS think of investing your IRA in real estate?

The IRS makes the following statement on their website "… because of administrative burdens, many IRA trustees do not allow IRA owners to invest IRA funds in real estate. IRA law does not prohibit investing in real estate but trustees are not required to offer real estate as an option."

Can my IRA purchase real estate I already own?

No. This would be considered a prohibited transaction (see IRC 4975). You many not purchase property that is owned by you or any other disqualified person (see below). You would need to purchase another piece of real estate that you don't already own.

Why does my current broker say I can't buy & hold real estate in my IRA?

Most likely because your current broker won't let you invest in real estate through their custodian. Just because that isn't something they offer doesn't mean that you can't do it; it just means that you can't do it through them. It is a limitation that your broker is placing on your IRA; NOT one that the IRS is placing on your IRA or your current broker may just be ignorant. Either way, you can invest in real estate.

What is the easiest way to buy real estate using my IRA?

The Self-directed IRA LLC is the way to get checkbook control over your IRA. A self-directed IRA account isn't enough. You will still need to get permission and have someone else sign off on all investments you want to make. If you are ready to be in control of your IRA, you need the Self-Directed IRA LLC.

Do I get complete control?

Having a self-directed IRA is one step toward obtaining complete control. To obtain a truly self-directed retirement account you need the Self-Directed IRA LLC. This is the structure that gives you checkbook control. When you simply establish an account with a self-directed custodian, you are still required to get permission from the custodian before making each investment.

This is time consuming, cumbersome and more expensive than it needs to be. With the Self-Directed IRA LLC you are then able to make investments the minute you decide to without getting permission from anyone. You have the checkbook. You are in control of your retirement money. We firmly believe that you are the best steward for your money. Nobody cares as much about your retirement as you do.

If I buy an income-producing rental property, what happens to the rental income?

The income goes back into the Self-Directed IRA LLC, and you retain the tax deferred or tax free status of the investment.

Can my Self-Directed IRA LLC get a loan and use my IRA money as the down payment if I don't have enough money in my IRA to purchase a piece of property outright?

Yes. You may use your IRA monies as the down payment and then have your Self-Directed IRA LLC get a loan for the balance.

However, you will not be able to personally guarantee the loan. It must be a non-recourse type of loan, which means that if your IRA fails to make payments, the only recourse the lender has, is against the property itself.

Further, there will be tax ramifications to doing so; UDFI (unrelated debt financed income) tax applies when a loan is obtained so you would want to confer with your tax professional about what forms would be necessary.

My IRA is small. May I personally co-invest with my IRA?

It is NOT a prohibited transaction for you to co-invest with your IRA. However, there are certain formalities that need to be adhered to, and there are some situations where it isn't advised.

Can my IRA co-invest with friends?

Yes. IRAs may purchase an undivided (and proportionate) interest in real estate.

Can I be the property manager of the real estate?

That depends. With just a self-directed IRA the answer is no. But with the Self-Directed IRA LLC you have the ability to manage the property, collect the rent and pay the bills. Unlike just having a self-directed IRA (which put restrictions on what you can do), the Self-Directed IRA LLC structure allows you to advertise for renters, collect and deposit the rent checks, pay the real estate bills, etc. This saves your IRA a lot of money and helps provide a more comfortable and prosperous retirement for you.

May I use my IRA funds to make improvements or renovations?

Yes. In fact, you must use IRA funds to make the improvements and pay all expenses associated with the property. All expenses of the property are paid with IRA funds, and all profits made on the property are returned to the IRA. This makes sense because it is an investment of the IRA.

Can I buy vacation property?

Yes. Doing so would NOT constitute a prohibited transaction. However, you cannot vacation there.

Can I buy my dream retirement home with my IRA and then live in it when I reach the age of retirement?

Yes. Your IRA would be the original owner. You would use your IRA money to make the purchase and maintain the property. Any rents generated would be returned to the IRA. However, upon reaching retirement age, the property could be distributed out to you. Of course, you would have to pay taxes on the distribution.

What are the advantages to using a Self-Directed IRA LLC when investing my IRA in real estate?

You can only receive checkbook control with the Self-Directed IRA LLC. With a self-directed custodian, you get more control than you get with a traditional custodian, but you still have to get permission from the custodian for every little thing you do. This is problematic, unnecessary and annoying. Further, with a time sensitive investment it puts you at a huge disadvantage - and what real estate purchases isn't time sensitive.

If you don't move quickly, you may miss out on a great opportunity.
Think of tax liens and tax deeds sold on the courthouse steps; you need to have checkbook control since payments are due after the auction is completed.

With the Self-Directed IRA LLC you have the checkbook, authority to write checks so you can make an investment without delay. This ensures that your IRA is able to make the best investments at the best prices.

Also with the Self-Directed IRA LLC your IRA will be subject to fewer and lower fees from the custodian than is typical with self-directed IRA that do not hold an LLC designation. Thus, there is more money for your retirement, which is the whole goal of an IRA.
You obtain the ability to manage the property, collect the rent and pay the bills. Unlike just having a self-directed IRA which put restrictions on what you can do, the Self-Directed IRA LLC structure allows you to advertise for

renters, collect and deposit the rent checks, pay the real estate bills, etc. This can save your IRA a lot of money and helps provide a more comfortable and prosperous retirement for you.

Can my Self-Directed IRA LLC get a mortgage on a piece of property?

Yes. The mortgage loan would need to be a non-recourse variety, meaning that if your IRA fails to make the payments, the only recourse the lending institution has is the property itself. Also, be aware that if your IRA obtains a loan, unrelated debt-financing income tax will apply.

Can my Self-Directed IRA LLC make loans to other individuals who want to buy real estate?

Absolutely. This is done frequently and it is a great investment for your IRA because the loan can be secured by the property.

Can I make a loan to my brother so that he can use the money as a down payment on a home?

Yes. According to IRC 4975, siblings are not included in the definition of disqualified persons. Thus, a loan to your brother would not be a prohibited transaction. Although some suggest that it was an error on the part of the IRS to omit siblings from the definition, they, nonetheless, were omitted and to the best of our knowledge, there has never been an IRS ruling to the contrary.

Can my Self-Directed IRA LLC make loans to a friend?

Absolutely. Friends are not disqualified persons under the Code, and therefore, your IRA can make a loan to them for whatever purpose of boat, airplane, hot tub,

home improvements, etc. Of course, you will want to make sure that there are proper formalities and reasonable terms to the loan.

Can my Self-Directed IRA LLC make loans to a real estate developer?

Yes. Your IRA can loan money to a real estate developer to finance the purchase of property or the development of property. Developers often look for private financing so it is a great way to get your IRA involved in real estate development. And because developers often pay an above market interest rate, the loan can be a great investment for your IRA.

Can my Self-Directed IRA LLC make loans to businesses or companies?

Sure. Your IRA can make a loan to any type of business. However, be aware that there are some restrictions on loan money to any business that you or any other disqualified person has an ownership interest in.

Do taxes and penalties apply when I take money out to buy real estate?

No. You DO NOT take money out to purchase real estate or anything else you want to buy.

It is just a purchase of your IRA or your Self-Directed IRA LLC. There are no taxes or penalties. Instead of buying 1000 shares of Microsoft or any other typical stock, your IRA is just making a different type of investment. The method of doing so is different but the tax ramifications are the same.

Are the gains that my Self-Directed IRA LLC makes taxable?

Not in most cases. If an IRA buys a piece of property and then sells it at a profit, the gains stay within the IRA. If you have a traditional IRA, the gains are tax-deferred. If you have a Roth IRA, the gains are tax-free. Note: you alter that result if you use leverage.

Are there any special taxes that apply when I use debt financing to purchase real estate?

Unrelated business taxable income (UBIT) would apply. Due to non-profit organizations encroachment on the business opportunities normally engaged in by taxable businesses, the IRS code was altered to include the provision in 1950.

Essentially, if a tax-exempt entity (e.g., non-profit) engages in a business that is unrelated to its primary purpose, any income derived from such business will be subject to UBIT. IRAs are also subject to UBIT if they conduct unrelated businesses that produce profits.

For example, if an IRA forms an LLC to buy and operate a dry cleaner or gas station, businesses obviously unrelated to the primary purpose of an IRA, the net income will be taxed as UBIT (at the trust tax rate because an IRA is considered a trust under the tax code in this purpose). The change in the code was intended to level the playing field between tax-exempt organizations and for-profit organizations conducting the same businesses.

Does it still make sense to leverage real estate?

Absolutely. Because of your increased buying power when you use leverage, the profits you make from the ability to use leverage can greatly outweigh the tax associated with the gains.

Can I invest outside of my state or outside the country?

Yes! Your IRA can invest outside of the U.S. There are many great investment opportunities in other countries.

What are IRA Prohibited Transactions?

Understanding what constitutes a prohibited transaction is very important when it comes to making investments within your IRA. The IRS defines a prohibited transaction as follows:

"Generally a prohibited transaction is any improper use of your IRA account or annuity by you, your beneficiary or any disqualified person. Disqualified persons include your fiduciary and members of your family (spouse, ancestor, linear descendant, and any spouse of linear descendant)." IRS Publication 590,

IRC 4975 is the section that lays out the rules on prohibited transactions. Prohibited transactions generally involve one of the following:

(1) Doing business with a disqualified person
(2) Benefiting someone other than the IRA
(3) Loaning money to a disqualified person
(4) Investing in a prohibited investment.

In plain English, prohibited transactions are those transactions that violate the basic intent of the IRA. Your IRA must receive the benefit rather than you. In other words, there can be no "self-dealing" transactions. However, there are many ways in which you can invest your IRA and not be in violation of the prohibited transaction law. When your IRA benefits, you benefit eventually because it is for your retirement.

What are IRA Prohibited Investments?

The Internal Revenue Code does not specifically authorize investments within an IRA; rather, the code outlines what types of investments are not allowed. The prohibited investments include: artwork, rugs, antiques, metals, gems, stamps, coins, beverages, stock in a S-Corporation, and certain other tangible personal property.

Who is a disqualified person?

The IRA holder and his or her spouse, the IRA holders ancestors, lineal descendants and their spouses; investment advisors and managers, any corporation, partnership, trust or estate in which the IRA holder has a 50% or greater interest; and anyone providing services to the IRA such as a trustee or custodian.

How am I a disqualified person?

It doesn't seem to make sense? There is a clear distinction between your IRA and you individually.

You and your IRA are not the same. Your IRA is a separate trust for your benefit when you retire.

What would be classified as Self-Dealing?

Self-dealing is using your IRA in transactions that in some way benefit you (or other disqualified persons) individually. The purpose of your IRA is to provide for your retirement. It is not intended to benefit you prior to retirement and distribution of the funds.

What are some types and examples of prohibited transactions and / or self-dealing transactions?

You can't purchase a home from your daughter or purchase a property from yourself that you already own. You can only invest in new properties and purchase properties from an individual who is not considered a disqualified person. A disqualified person is a person who is a direct descendant.

You purchase a vacation home, hunting property or a golf course as an investment for your IRA but you yourself cannot personally use it. All the purchases made by the IRA LLC MUST be for investment purposes only.

You cannot perform maintenance on a property that your IRA owns and pay yourself for work that you do on the property such as repairing a leaking faucet.

Can I buy a business with my Self-Directed IRA LLC?

Yes, you can buy a business with your IRA money via the Self-Directed IRA LLC. Please contact us for details.

Can I invest in an existing business?

Yes. This can be done as the purchase of stock as a loan to the business.

What about S-Corporations, can I form an IRA S-Corp?

S-Corporations do not allow IRAs as investors; they only allow individuals as investors. Therefore, it isn't so much that IRAs are prohibited from investing in S-Corporations rather that S-Corporations don't permit having an IRA as a shareholder. It is likely that the investment of the IRA would revoke the sub-s status of the corporation.

Can I buy Stocks, CDs, Bonds, Options, in my CHECKBOOK IRA LLC?

Yes. There is no sense in letting your retirement funds sit on the sidelines while you are looking for real estate investments. You can invest in publicly traded stocks, CDs, mutual funds, annuities, bonds, stock options, futures, etc.

If you are an active day trader, with checkbook control you will be able to trade in your IRA in a manner that your current broker does not allow using the Self-Directed IRA LLC. For example, you probably have asked your broker if you can buy or sell Options (Calls and Puts). Or maybe you would like to write covered calls or do spreads and have been told 'no'. The Self-Directed IRA LLC allows you to trade your way.

I have a 401K with an old employer. Can I move it into the Self-Directed IRA LLC?

Yes. You can move these 401K funds into the Self-Directed IRA LLC. We do it all the time. We can facilitate the rollover so that you can unlock those funds for your next real estate purchase.

Is the transfer a taxable event?

No, and neither is a direct rollover.

Can I move it into the Self-Directed IRA LLC?

I have a 401K with my current employer. Depending on the 401K-plan document for your current employer, it will specify what you can do, but most of the time you cannot move money from a 401K plan if you are currently working for the company. However, in some cases you might be able to unlock a portion of your 401K funds and self direct those funds for real estate investing purposes. It is worth investigating.

Contact your company retirement plan representative to obtain the plan document. You will want to check the plan document and see if you can do an "in-service transfer". If you can, then read the details. You might be able to transfer all or a part of your IRA to a Self-Directed IRA for investing.

I have several IRAs and old 401Ks. Can I combine them?

Yes. They can all be combined and then invested into your Self-Directed IRA LLC so that your buying power is maximized. The only restriction is on 401(k) accounts; you generally must no longer work for the employer. You can usually combine multiple retirement accounts into one account.

Or in the event that they can't be combined, such as the case of a traditional IRA and a Roth IRA, they can still be invested into the same Self-Directed IRA LLC so that you still have maximum buying power.

How do I get started?

Call Asset Exchange Group (AEG) at 866-683-5228.

Does AEG offer checkbook control to investors?

Yes.

Does AEG allow investments in LLC's and LPs?

Yes.

Can I invest in an LLC I manage?

Yes.

If I don't want to be the manager of my IRA's LLC, can I authorize access to another person (my accountant, for example)?

Yes.

Can I partner with my IRA, and if so, what are your rules?

Yes. AEG will need to create a separate LLC for the partnership.

Can my IRA partner with another unrelated individual on investment properties?

Absolutely.

Can my IRA pay for pre-construction reservations I intend to assign or simultaneously close on?

Yes.

Can my IRA invest in secured and unsecured notes?

Yes.

Does AEG have the flexibility to consider unique transactions? Yes

Can I manage rental properties owned by my IRA, and if so, is there a limit to how many?

Yes, and there is no limit.

Must I hire a bookkeeper for rental properties owned by my IRA?

No.

Are you bonded for theft and fraud?

The asset is held by the LLC, not by AEG.

Are funds that are not invested but remain in my IRA insured? Typically yes. Since the client has checkbook control, the funds are in an FDIC insured bank account.

Does AEG have any litigation ongoing or pending?

No.

Does AEG have an audited annual report available?

No.

Does AEG permit you debt-financed properties?

Yes.

Does AEG permit you foreign real estate?

Yes.

What is your review process of limited partnerships?

AEG drafts the LPs with tax attorneys. Typically the custodians have no say in the content and cannot make a judgment upon any instrument such as this.

What are the most common problems in real estate transactions?

People use funds incorrectly and/or title the property incorrectly.

Does AEG offer any advice on investment vehicles or individual investments?

Yes. AEG can, but custodians cannot offer advice!!!

Is AEG independent of products they recommended?

Yes.

Does AEG have a complaint procedure?

Yes.

Does AEG have any testimonials?

Yes.

What sets AEG apart from the rest?

AEG offers support beyond the custodian level. You'll find the answers from the custodians you have contacted will be considerably different than those we provided for you. The custodian is a product to AEG. AEG will find the best IRA strategy to meet your needs, and can also structure the deal so you and the IRA holders are shielded from the IRS. AEG offers the four following benefits:

1. Checkbook control
2. You make your investment decisions without custodial intervention
3. Litigation protection of the IRA
4. Lowest possible custodial costs

Is AEG willing to send a representative to conduct a real estate IRA workshop for signing up members of a group to your company?

Yes.

GLOSSARY & WEB LINKS

Refer to web link sources for additional information.

- 1031 Exchange – A transaction in which the tax on the gain is deferred until some future date.
  www.1031.org/about1031/faq.htm
- Adjusted Gross Income (AGI) – The amount used to calculate an individual's income tax liability; one's income after certain adjustments are made, but before standardized and itemized deductions and personal exemptions are made.
  www.investorwords.com/112/Adjusted_Gross_Income.html
- Administrator – A financial institution that holds funds (custodial services), provides reports to the IRS, and acts as a watchdog to ensure IRA compliance.
  www.myrealestateira.com/iraglossary.html
- Asset – Anything owned which can produce future economic benefit.
  http://en.wikipedia.org/wiki/Asset
- Attorney groups – Attorneys that understand the requirements to properly structure and implement an instrument so that it is compliant.
  www.myrealestateira.com/iraglossary.html
- Bear Market – A prolonged period in which investment prices fall accompanied by widespread pessimism. Bear markets usually occur when

the economy is in a recession and unemployment is high, or when inflation is rising quickly.
www.investorwords.com/443/bear_market.html

- Bridging loans – Short-term loans often used by purchasers of a property who need funds for a limited period of time. e.g., until they sell their existing home.
www.moneyextra.com/dictionary/bridging-loans-moneyextra-003585.html

- Catch-up contribution – A provision that permits 401k plan participants age 50 and over to make additional "catch-up" contributions: Effective for plan years starting on or after January 1, 2002.
www.401khelpcenter.com/catch-up_contributions.html

- Checkbook control – The ability to write a check for any desired investment within IRS compliance directives.

  There is often no requirement to report to the administrator.
www.myrealestateira.com/iraglossary.html

- Contributions – Payments made to the IRA.

- Contribution Limits – The maximum dollar amount individuals are allowed to deposit into their IRA each year.
http://beginnersinvest.about.com/cs/iras/a/iracontribution.htm

- Custodian – A financial institution that acts a record keeper for retirement accounts, and is required to follow IRS compliance directives. An administrator and custodian are often the same institution. www.myrealestateira.com/iraglossary.html

- Distributions – A withdrawal from a qualified retirement plan.
- Employer Pension Plan – Generally speaking, there are two types of pension plans: defined benefit plans and defined contribution plans. A defined benefit plan promises you a specified monthly benefit at retirement. The plan may state this promised benefit as an exact dollar amount, such as $100 per month at retirement.

  Or, more commonly, it may calculate a benefit through a plan formula that considers such factors as salary and service - for example, one percent of your average salary for the last five years of employment for every year of service with your employer.

  A defined contribution plan, on the other hand, does not promise you a specific amount of benefits at retirement. In these plans, you or your employer (or both) contribute to your individual account under the plan, sometimes at a set rate, such as five percent of your earnings annually.

  These contributions generally are invested on your behalf. You will ultimately receive the balance in your account, which is based on contributions plus or minus investment gains or losses. The value of your account will fluctuate due to changes in the value of your investments. Examples of defined contribution plans include 401(k) plans, 403(b) plans, employee stock ownership plans, and profit-sharing plans. www.dol.gov/ebsa/faqs/faq_consumer_pension.html#

- Employee Retirement Security Act (ERISA),
- Equity – The meaning of equity depends very much on the context. In general, you can think of equity as ownership in any asset after all debts associated with that asset are paid off. For example, a car or house with no outstanding debt is considered the owner's equity since he or she can readily sell the items for cash. Stocks are equity because they represent ownership of a company, whereas bonds are classified as debt because they represent an obligation to pay and not ownership of assets. www.investopedia.com/terms/e/equity.asp
- Hedge Funds – An aggressively managed investment portfolio that uses advanced investment strategies such as leverage, long, short and derivative positions in both domestic and international markets with the goal of generating high returns. www.answers.com/topic/hedge-fund
- National Association of Financial and Estate Planning (NAFEP) – A privately held, for profit organization based in Salt Lake City, Utah. Its primary business is two fold:
    - Provision of estate planning consultation and documents through a nationwide network of professional sales associates
    - A training and certification program for professionals known as Certified Estate Advisor®(CEA®). NAFEP professional sales associates

are attorneys, CPAs or financial planners who have completed the CEA®.

www.nafep.com/nafep%20info/nafep- info_home.htm

- Non-Elective Contributions – A type of contribution made by an employer to each eligible employee's employer-sponsored retirement plan. The contribution is not based on salary reduction contributions made by the employee. www.investopedia.com/terms/n/non-electivecontribution.asp
- Non-traditional or alternative investment assets or products – Broadly speaking, an alternative investment are any investment other than the traditional investments such as publicly traded stocks, bonds and mutual funds. The actual definition varies among financial institutions and investors, but it generally includes hedge funds, real estate, venture capital and derivatives. www.investopedia.com/articles/retirement/06/AlternativeInvestments.asp
- Pass-through Tax Entity – The profit or loss generated by the business which is reflected on the owner's personal income tax return. This helps the business owner avoid the double taxation of paying first corporate tax on profits and then personal income tax on distributions of profits. www.corporate.com/llc-definition.jsp
- Penalty-free Withdrawals – Early withdrawals from the IRA that are not subject to the 10% early distribution penalty. The IRS waiver applies only

in certain circumstances.
www.investopedia.com/articles/retirement/02/111202.asp

- Plan Document – A contract between the IRA holder and the financial institution that explains the provisions of the IRA. The document includes items such as allowable investments, contribution limits, and rules for deducting an IRA contribution, distribution rules and the rights of the IRA owner. An IRA is not considered 'established' until the IRA holder signs the agreement.
www.answers.com/topic/ira-adoption-agreement-and-plan-document

- Portable Plan Benefits – Ability to retain the amount you have contributed to your account when you change jobs.

- Re-characterization – An action that reverses the conversion of an IRA from one type to another. For example, the conversion of a traditional IRA into a Roth IRA may be re-characterized, returning the relevant funds to the traditional IRA.
www.investorwords.com/5756/recharacterization.html

- Real Estate Investment Trust (REIT) – A security that sells like a stock on the major exchanges and invests in real estate directly, either through properties or mortgages.
www.investopedia.com/terms/r/reit.asp

- Tax advantaged vehicle – Any type of investment program that strives to reduce the impact of taxes on investor earnings. There are tax-advantaged investment vehicles in just about every asset category.

  "Tax-advantaged" generally refers to two different kinds of investments: tax-deferred and tax-free. Tax-deferred investments simply defer taxes until investment earnings are withdrawn, at which time the investor is more likely to be in a lower tax bracket. Tax-free investments produce earnings that are actually free not only from federal taxes, but sometimes from federal and state taxes.
  www.huntingtonfunds.com/resource/tax_advantaged.asp

- Tax deductible – An item or expense subtracted from adjusted gross income to reduce the amount of income subject to tax, e.g. mortgage interest, state and local taxes, un-reimbursed business expenses, and charitable contributions.
  www.investorwords.com/4889/tax_deductible.html

- Tax-deferred – Income whose taxes can be postponed until a later date, for example, IRA, 401(k), Keogh Plan, annuity, Savings Bond and Employee Stock Ownership Plan.
  www.investorwords.com/4891/tax_deferred.html

- Tax Lien – A claim imposed by the federal government to liquidate a person's property until the tax and debt owed is fully paid. Tax liens can be

purchased from the government in the form of an investment.
www.investopedia.com/terms/t/taxlien.asp

- Traditional Investment Assets or Products – Stocks, bonds, mutual funds, annuities, life insurance policies.
- Vesting – The process by which employees accrue non-forfeitable rights over employer contributions that are made to the employee's qualified retirement plan account. Generally, non-forfeitable rights accrue based on the number of years of service performed by the employee. The exact requirements are specified in the plan document, which also contains any applicable regulations.
www.investopedia.com/terms/v/vesting.asp

Daniel Cordoba, CEA

THE KNOWLEDGE LEADER ON ASSET EXCHANGE STRATEGIES

Speaking Engagements
Seminar Programs
Personal Consultations
Executive Retirement Planning

Speaker Topics
Exercise Tax Favorable Strategies
Self-Directed Retirement Planning
Leverage Asset & Entity Advantages

Designations
B.A. in Business Management, University of Phoenix: Certified Estate Advisor (CEA) awarded by National Association of Financial and Estate Planning

Professional Licenses
Texas Department of Insurance Life and Accident Insurance, Texas Real Estate Commission Instructor, Real Estate Finance and Real Estate Investments, NASD Investor Education on Professional Designations

Contact Information
www.danielcordoba.com
info@danielcordoba.com
866-683-5228

Recognized Leader in education offerings for self-directed IRA Investing; Principal of Asset Exchange Group, LLC; President of Asset Exchange Strategies, LLC; Founder of NATFI, National Association of Tax Favorable Investing

In Detail – Daniel Cordoba is recognized as the expert in asset exchange strategies including self-directed retirement investing. He is quoted and featured in numerous high-end media, and continues to be sought out for speaking engagements, advice, and consulting services. He is the Author of the Texas Real Estate Commission approved real estate course: Tax Favorable Real Estate Transactions.

How He Presents – Daniel is a frequent speaker at national investor groups; an instructor to high producing real estate agents, investment talk radio shows, and television news broadcasts. His powerful presentations are packed with a rich source of actionable information, which he expresses with clarity and precision.

Media - Daniel is quoted in Kiplinger's Magazine, Wall Street Journal, Forbes, OnWall Street, Women's Wall Street, Reality Times, CPA journals and other notable online and print media.

"The IRS spends God knows how much of your tax money on these toll-free information hot lines staffed by IRS employees whose idea of a dynamite tax tip is that you should print neatly.

If you ask them a real tax question, such as how you can cheat, they're useless. So, for guidance you want to look to big business. Big business never pays a nickel in taxes, according to Ralph Nader who represents a big consumer organization that never pays a nickel in taxes... "

Dave Barry 1947 - 'Sweating Out Taxes'

ISBN 978-0-6152-2308-7

Asset Exchange Strategies Publishing, LLC

Created and Printed in the United States of America

www.assetexchangestrategies.com